Giving it the Bigun

Paul 'Bigun' Ashbee

NEW HAVEN PUBLISHING LTD

Published 2019
New Haven Publishing
www.newhavenpublishingltd.com
newhavenpublishing@gmail.com

All Rights Reserved
The rights of Paul Ashbee, as the author of this work, have been asserted in accordance with the Copyrights, Designs and Patents Act 1988.
No part of this book may be re-printed or reproduced or utilized in any form or by any electronic, mechanical or other means, now unknown or hereafter invented, including photocopying, and recording, or in any information storage or retrieval system, without the written permission of the Author and Publisher.

Cover design ©Pete Cunliffe
pcunliffe@blueyonder.co.uk

Copyright © 2019 Paul Ashbee
All rights reserved
ISBN: 978-1-912587-22-3

To my Nana and Grandad Kay, and Grandad and Nana Ashbee, who are no longer with us, RIP

Contents

The Mancunian Way	9
Short Sleeve Steve and the Nine Stone Cowboy	17
Spiked Island	27
Pretty Clean	33
Life on the Cliff	39
And Four Becomes Five	48
You've Got to Make it Happen	58
A Hurricane Comes to Town	64
Fergie Puts the Boot in	73
Georgian England	101
Reality Strikes	112
Time Waits for no Man	117
My Mate, Goldenbollocks	123
Most Rock n Roll Legal Aid Ever	132
When Love Breaks Down	142
Super Mario	154
Afterword	165

Preface

Greetings my brethren and welcome to my wonderful world. Guess I should introduce myself. My name is Paul Ashbee although I am more widely referred to around Manchester, England as the 'Big Un' and so shall be the case throughout this book. This name was bestowed upon me due to my large physical size rather than any 'attitude' or 'aggression' I may give out. My large frame began developing in my early teens when I seemed to have to lower my head to talk to my classmates, and to be honest, I like the name. Always gets a giggle.

So, what's with the book Bigun? Well, I guess this book is born from my introduction to the world in Tony McCarroll's autobiography *Oasis – The Truth*. Tony was a founding member of the musical group Oasis and I guess his book gave a glimpse of the rather twisted and generally fuckin chaotic Mancunian world I live in. Since, I've been approached by numerous publishers all wanting me to tell my tale, so here I am!

I hope you find my recollections of times past in sunny Manchester both entertaining and thought provoking. I hope it triggers memories of glorious times in both music and sport. Along the way in this ramble we call life I've made many friends whom I have both helped and hindered, guided and led astray. This is for them as well. Applauds to some and apologies to others. Right, anyway, enough of this, let's get the fuckin show on the road!

- Paul Ashbee

Chapter One
The Mancunian Way

The few biographies I've taken the time to read all begin with a long, in-depth view of a child's wondrous introduction into this world, their formative exploration into a new environment, the joys of attachment with Mother and Father, making educational friendships that last a lifetime, learning and experiencing this big, brave, beautiful world, blah, blah, blah..... Well, I've decided to scratch that bit and run you through it all in the next few pages.

You see, I'm pretty sure you're not reading this book to hear about the time I looked after the next door neighbour's cat whilst she went on holiday to Rhyl, although to be honest I did end up losing the cat whilst pissed on the Waltzers at the local fair and had to replace it with... shit, I'm doing what I promised not to... anyway, here goes...

I was born on New Year's Eve, December 1966 at Withington Hospital in South Manchester. My old fella told me that he held me aloft that day and my screams could be heard as far away as Levenshulme, where we lived.

Barry and Jean Ashbee, my parents, were hard working, decent people, but like most dwelling in the working-class districts of Manchester in the seventies they had to work hard to put the chicken on the table come Sunday.

As well as the arrival of my big, bouncing self, my parents later also had two other children to look after, my younger sisters, Gaynor and Suzanne, who I was possessive and protective of. So, after the nurse had given me a good slap, I was wrapped back in my baby blue blanket and driven home to Levenshulme in the family's clapped out Morris Minor.

I grew up in West Point. Not the American military academy but rather the west point of Levenshulme, Manchester. Although there would be no official boundary marked on a map everybody knew where West Point started and where West Point finished. And for good reason. We protected our patch and had gained quite a reputation in doing so and heaven help any unsuspecting non-locals caught wandering our streets. With West Point being a small enclave trapped between Levenshulme and Longsight you either acted tough or you got trampled over. It was that simple. Or so it seemed at the time.

My father is incredibly proud of one thing in his life. This is the fact that the family lineage can be traced directly back to William the Conqueror. He still offers me this advice regularly:

'We have to conquer many things in life. Some stand before us and some live within.'

It's always stuck with me, that.

I attended school firstly at Wuthering Heights Primary and then later at Bollocks College High. I enjoyed my time at school although I was, like most, more interested in girls and football than algebra or physics.

My love for football was born at an early age. After an introduction from my father I became a devout follower of Manchester United Football Club, which helped me get to socialise on a wider scale, and I soon became friends with other United lads in different schools all over Levenshulme and Longsight.

I guess I was lucky enough to experience United in all their glories, from the mud splattered fields of the seventies with Buchan and the Greenhoffs to the Class of 92 when we defeated all before us.

Unlike some United fans though, I do have an affinity with Manchester City. It's just hard not to. A lot of my family and friends supported the blue half and that's just the way I was.

I had three close friends during my formative school years, John Morrin, John Scott and one Paul Arthurs, and it must be said, we were a bit of an odd crowd, and I guess this is where my story begins.

John Morrin was from a large Irish family so was surrounded by a band of brothers with a reputation for being able to take care of themselves. John himself was a bit more reserved than his brothers but had the same pugilistic abilities. He was short but squarely built and was a fearsome and loyal friend.

John Scott, or Johnno as he was more often referred to, was quite the opposite to Mr Morrin in his physique. Tall and slender, he was quick in wit and considered himself a bit of a player. If I recall correctly, I think I remember Face from *The A Team* being a bit of a role model for Johnno.

And then we have Paul Benjamin Arthurs, known as Bonehead. Paul was the product of two more Irish immigrants and had one brother and one sister making them the smallest Irish family in Manchester. Paul had an infectious sense of humour and a permanent smile. He had the ability to lighten a dark situation with his boundless enthusiasm and comic intervention although sometimes it would land us all in trouble.

We were as firm a set of friends as you would find, and we journeyed through childhood together. After school we would play in the local parks and have tea at each other's houses.

Much of our time was filled with all things football. We watched football, we talked about football and we played football. Later in life that passion was occasionally known to spill over into the odd bit of football hooliganism but never anything too serious.

After a fairly normal early schooling filled with laughter, mischievousness and them pesky girls we all headed to high school. Bonehead had always displayed a natural eagerness to learn so unlike the rest of us he attended Realposh College School while the rest of us went to a normal comprehensive.

This didn't deter our friendship though and at about fourteen years of age we began getting into the music scene of Manchester. We attended local concerts; Johnno joined us when he could, but the majority of the time it was just me and Bonehead. And boy was it a love affair.

It was the unfortunate and tragic demise of Joy Division and the musical rebirth of the band as New Order that brought about such. I consider New Order to be vastly underrated in regard to their influence on not only the Mancunian music scene but UK electronic music in general.

I remember dancing to early New Order with Bonehead in his bedroom. Even then, before the whole 'Madchester' scene, we always had this feeling that something was going to happen, was going to explode, do you know what I mean? It was like there was a movement and it was heading for something historic and explosive. It was probably like when rock and roll came about. The youth then must've felt like a change was in the air. A movement. A renaissance, if you like.

Bonehead was always talking about music and he was always playing instruments. Wherever he went he'd have a mouth organ or a spoon or whatever, and he could play anything. In the not too distant future, he would form a band and would become, to me, the most integral part in the creation of that band's sound. Everything about it, the vibe, the attitude, for me personally, it came from him.

We loved our local bands but of course we weren't regionally blinkered. We were bang into music that blared from cities other than Manchester, but I guess you gravitate to those you can relate most to and so, in my home city, we were the kids in the proverbial sweet shop.

Well, I loved everything about the music scene. I loved the bands and the gigs. I loved being in a large crowd watching an established band or being one of a handful of people watching a new band. I just fell in love with it and all that it offered.

Because of that, I kept pleading with Bonehead for us to start up our own band. I really wanted a slice of that musical pie. I wanted to feast on it: the coolness, the fame, the girls and all the trappings.

Unfortunately for me Bonehead always pointed out that I couldn't sing or play an instrument. I'd hold my huge, clumsy hands up, which look like a few pounds of sausages and quite obviously could never play a guitar even if they wanted to. But I knew I could be involved in some way and vowed to make sure that I was if an opportunity came up.

And so onwards we marched. The four of us finished our educations and were thrown out into eighties Britain. Wasn't that pleasant if I recall rightly. I was at a loose end in terms of what career to pursue. Bonehead decided, like his father before him, that plastering might offer him a living and so planned to begin work with his father.

Shortly after, me and Bonehead were sat in the park drinking White Lightning. We had only five pounds between us which wasn't really enough to quench the thirst for entertainment that we had. It was common around West Point: sometimes you had money, sometimes you didn't; and when you didn't you went in search of those that did. Then when they didn't and you did, you looked after them.

We'd heard on the grapevine that there was a party nearby held by my sister's mate, and we were obviously interested in crashing said party, having nothing else to do and no money to do it with.

We tracked down where the party was happening, and it was in a more affluent area of Manchester called Chorlton. We'd figured there'd be plenty to drink there and with the White Lightning heightening, we rocked up to this massive Victorian house. We were looking for some action, whatever that action may be.

Slurring to each other to check it out, we sussed out where the optimum point would be to have a nosy through the window. We plumped on one of the front ones, a big old thing that was awkward to get to but looked into what we thought must be the front room. The party room in our stuporous opinions.

We traipsed through the grass and the bushes and flowers that were in front of the house and I hoisted myself up to look through this big old bay window.

'Bone'ead, have a look at this, mate,' I urged him, and told him to get up on his tiptoes and have a peep through. He muttered something and strutted forward confidently. I was still trying to peer through when out of the corner of my eye I saw him go to look in the window before suddenly disappearing. Poof! Like a magic act.

I'd had so much cheap booze that my addled brain couldn't comprehend what had happened for a while, until I heard a groan from below me.

In front of the window was a hole that neither of us had seen. Bonehead had fallen through the opening where there should have been a grate that covers the recess for a cellar window. In the old days it would have been the opening for the coal to be poured down into the cellar. What it offered for our Bonehead was a massive hole to not see.

Like a thrown mannequin he lay ten feet down, strewn in the recess. He was wailing due to a twisted ankle and looked a right sorry state. Thing is, with Bonehead he would've been laughing were it not for the pain. That said, if it hadn't been for him being pissed up, he probably would've been in a lot more pain than he was. They say that about drunks in accidents, don't they?

I tried to pull him out of there, but I was just laughing, and all my strength was going with each wave of giggles. In the end, I had to knock on the door and introduce myself to the hosts and guests of the party, and then in the same breath ask for their help in getting my good friend out of the hole in front of the window that we'd just been spying through.

They were great about it and set to negotiating an injured and drunk Bonehead out of the depths. It took about four of us to get him out and I literally pissed myself a little bit from laughing so hard. He came out of there looking like an old tramp, all dishevelled with his arms scraped up and looking very sorry for himself indeed.

Still, it only took a couple of drinks to make him feel better and we partied on through the night, with him hobbling about on a twisted ankle. The man is as mad as a box of frogs.

The following Wednesday afternoon in Manchester, we all had nothing to do and went to pick up Bonehead from his house in West Point Park. Out he limped holding his guitar, and he was soon strumming in the park and drinking.

Easily and swiftly bored, we decided to head down to The Old Cock, a pub in Didsbury just down the road. It was a nice day, going on for evening by this time, and it wasn't raining so we all sat outside with our beers. Bonehead got playing on his guitar again and we supped as we listened, sat around on benches.

Before long, we all felt the warm and fuzzy glow that you get when it's summer and alcohol is flowing; and before we knew it, we were singing along with Bonehead.

The landlady at the time was a nice woman, and a few songs in she threw open the window upstairs and listened before telling us how lovely it all sounded. It did. She may have been drunk, I know lots of us were, but however you slice it, people were happy and that's never a bad thing. She told us to carry on while she listened upstairs while putting her make up on.

In that fluid way that nights like that go, a couple of us decided to head up to the airport. I have no idea why, but we were young, foolish and thought, 'Fuck it, let's go to the airport.'

Bonehead had his guitar and wasn't afraid to use it. In that bit where you go through to departures, just before you hit customs, he sat his arse down and started strumming away on his guitar and singing. I didn't know what to do with myself, so decided to head off to the toilets and rid myself of some of the pints I'd been drinking.

I swear to god, when I came back a few minutes later, Bonehead had a crowd of about a hundred people gathered around him, all singing along to the tune he was playing.

And as if that wasn't enough to deal with, there was the issue of WHAT he was playing. He'd only gone full Cliff Richard and was belting out 'We're all going on a summer holiday' at the top of his lungs, with all the happy-go-lucky travellers singing along with him.

I stood there, mouth open, watching the spectacle before me, and continued to watch as the airport security grabbed him and told him to stop. They'd also clocked me, and came over, grabbed me as well and frogmarched us out of the airport. We were in fits of giggles of course at the whole thing, and Bonehead's only concern was that his guitar didn't get damaged. It didn't, and luckily for us all he got to play another day.

There was to be a lifetime of guitar playing and high-jinx in store for Bonehead. The more fun side of life suited him, but as always in Manchester there were those that didn't exactly see it that way.

We had a few scrapes and roll-arounds along the way but to be honest I'd seen a lot more vicious and intimidating kids on my somewhat limited travels, so I normally guided us away from any potential confrontations. This streetwise attitude served me well in my formative years and saved my bacon on a number of following occasions.

Unfortunately, the halcyon days of youth are not permanent, and I suppose my natural inclination to be a bit of a 'boy' was always going to end badly. And it did, as I found myself sitting in Her Majesty's Prison Manchester, more commonly known as Strangeways, in 1989, aged 23.

Chapter Two
Short Sleeve Steve and the Nine Stone Cowboy

So, the judge lifts his head and with one eye slightly askew looks down his prolonged, elderly nose at me. It was unmasked contempt. Doesn't matter what gets said from here on in, I knew it wasn't good news. I felt sick to the stomach and his voice became distant and unreal.

'I have no hesitation in ridding the British streets of an individual such as yourself, Mr Ashbee. I suggest you spend the next twelve months considering the consequences of your actions in the vainest hope it might lead to a change in your ways. I very much doubt such but in God we trust.'

You've got to be fucking kidding me. Twelve months? For defending myself against an unknown assailant? In fact, two unknown assailants. What had been a slightly intoxicated amble home one sunny September evening had taken a turn when I was approached by two men at the bottom of Matthews Lane, Levenshulme.

After they had tried to grab me and I had given the tallest one a bit of a right hook which sent him spiralling onto Stockport Road, the remaining attacker made a lunge for me, so I sent him one right on the bridge of his nose. His eyes widened as he slumped backwards and ended in a sitting position with blood spouting from the front of his face. This was the moment that the first unknown assailant made himself known by showing me his warrant card and stating,

'Police, you silly cunt.'

Whoops. The obvious lights and sirens descended, and I spent a whole night paying for what I considered a fine display of self defence. It seemed that the two undercover policemen had been looking for a man that fitted my description. It also seemed that they had identified themselves by shouting very loudly that they were police officers before they tried to accost me. Yeah right, I must have missed that bit.

Anyway, the fact that the judge simply dismissed any claims that I had acted in self-defence led to what was a genuine misunderstanding being twisted into an all-out assault on two of Her Majesty's finest. So, dependant on behaviour, at least the next six months of my life would be spent behind sixteen-feet thick concrete walls. Fuckin great.

After I was carted off from the court I was quickly into the system. I had always been a bit canny growing up. The streets taught you such. You kept your mouth tight shut and your eyes and ears wide open. Still, I was only twenty three years of age and open to intimidation. I quickly decided that I needed to find myself a pal. This process was sped up somewhat when I was introduced to my new cell mate. He was waiting at the doorway to my cell when I arrived.

'So, you're me new roommate?'

I was surprised to hear the ring of cockney tones; I had naively expected to be placed with a fellow Mancunian, like the system might try to match you up through likes and common interests. You could say I was right at the bottom of my learning curve.

'Certainly am, my mate. They call me Bigun.' I smiled and stretched out my hand, which was warmly shaken.

'My name is Steve but in here they call me Short Sleeve Steve.' I looked at his arms, covered by long shirt sleeves, as he explained:

'There's more than one Steve and I arrived in a short-sleeved Bermuda shirt. That's how things work in this gaff.'

'Jesus. What do you think they'll call me?'

'Won't be fucking Bigun, I can promise you that.'

And he was right. My huge frame became much less relevant when I was surrounded by men that were twice my size. Short Sleeve Steve was a stand-up guy. We would spend twelve months arguing whether the Jam should have become the Style Council or if Manchester United were a bigger club than his beloved Chelsea.

This period of my life shaped me in many different ways. I knew I was a chancer, but I never considered myself 'evil' and where I now found myself left me understanding exactly what 'evil' was.

Strangeways was straining under the pressures of government cuts and overcrowding. It was a very hostile and dangerous place to reside. There was a constant undercurrent of unease and anger at our sub-human treatment, which eventually led to the infamous Strangeways Riots. I had not picked a good time to get myself put down.

Bonehead, John and Johnno came to visit me though, right from the start. I would catch up with Bonehead about which bands he'd been to watch, and he would tell me about anything new he had heard. At the time he was waxing lyrical about the Happy Mondays and The Stone Roses, who were at the forefront of a whole new wave of bands emerging in Manchester. I had already been to watch The Stone Roses in Warrington before being incarcerated but it seemed that now things were really lifting off for them.

Bonehead's visits and musical news didn't really lift my spirits though. Instead they made me even more angry with myself for getting locked up.

One saving grace whilst in the clink was the fact that I had been banged up with a long streak of a man named Declan.

When I first spotted Declan on the wing, if I'm honest, I had tried to steer clear of him. Declan was in his early sixties. He still stood at well over six feet but was built like a pipe cleaner. I reckoned he'd have to run around in the shower to get wet.

I had first encountered Declan in the Midway pub in Levenshulme, some five years earlier. He would stand at the bar dressed head to toe in authentic cowboy gear. Yes, seriously. He had the waistcoat, frilly shirt, dusty trousers, boots, spurs and even a Stetson.

The most worrying part about the outfit though had to be the old leather gun belt that hung from his waist and, more lethally, the two shiny pistols that sat either side of his thighs. I'm not shitting you. This was the eighties and for some insane reason in Levenshulme this situation was deemed totally acceptable by the locals. Even when on occasion, in the middle of a pub fight, Declan would whip out his guns and fire blank bullets wildly into the crowd, leaving an acrid smell and smoke in the air. The gunshots were terrifyingly loud and normally came with a slurred 'yee-hah' from the Irish cowboy. The locals would laugh and raise their glasses while the non-locals would cower under tables or tear arse out the doors. It really was a sight to behold.

After a number of warnings by the local constabulary, which went ignored by the renegade, outlaw cowboy, Declan had his gun removed and himself placed in Strangeways. It was here that he was rather aptly named The Nine Stone Cowboy.

Me, Steve and Declan made for a strange mix. A young Mancunian, a middle-aged Cockney barrow-boy and a crazed Irish pensioner. Not the beginnings of group love you might think but for some reason the dynamic worked, and the nights passed quickly.

Declan's stories, infectious laughter and constant optimism rubbed off on both me and Steve and I actually started to enjoy my time inside.

Things really took a turn for the better though when one day I was joined by Johnno - and I don't mean in the visiting room. He had experienced an altercation not dissimilar to my own and had also received a twelve month slap for such. We managed to get ourselves padded up together and would swap visitors when John and Bonehead came. During my time inside a lot of my friends from outside passed through, including Brendan Murray, the phantom toilet paper lighter.

When it was time for me to leave Strangeways, I can honestly say that I didn't want to. I had become accustomed to the nightly fun and general camaraderie that sometimes a prison wing can offer.

Nevertheless, just under twelve months after my arrival, a slimline, repentant me was released back upon the streets of Manchester, and I didn't really expect what was waiting for me. There was a whole new musical explosion going on.

The house scene was taking off massively throughout the UK, but nowhere more so than in Manchester; we all felt very much a part of that musical explosion. The Hacienda was doing historical things and became famous worldwide. Or infamous, depending on your point of view.

If you've never heard of The Hacienda, then where the hell have you been? The Hacienda was a nightclub. It became huge during the Madchester years of the late eighties and early nineties; and was even labelled the most famous club in the world by *Newsweek* magazine.

It opened in 1982, and had years of financial problems and controversy, but managed to survive until 1997. Most of the time that it was open it was kept afloat by cash injections from record sales from my favourite band, New Order, who part-owned the club. When the rave scene fully kicked off, The Hacienda was associated with its rise and that of acid house.

I saw loads of famous people there. Footballers, pop stars and actors. I even saw Madonna there in 1986. She had just released or was about to release *True Blue*, so was at the time extremely well known across the globe. We later all went back to an after party in the early hours after clubbing, and Madonna was there as well. It was at a house in Chorlton and I remember staring across the room at the cocky American girl with the trampy clothes on.

Club-wise, there were different venues around town that specialised in different music and had, until the late eighties, been mostly frequented by either wholly black or wholly white people. Manchester didn't see it like that: music was music and we wanted to be involved in all of it. Manchester had always tried to introduce different genres of music within clubs that had a certain specific vibe to them. The Hacienda was a prime example of being a catalyst for that, and we took it upon ourselves to introduce some funk into the mix elsewhere.

So, dance music was huge, people were heading off to Ibiza as that blew up; and, very close to my heart, New Order had just released their album *Technique*. By the time this album came out they were far more upbeat and they too were influenced by the Balearic sounds of Ibiza making their way into the Hacienda. They even recorded the album in Ibiza. They were crazy and exciting days.

Our 'one world, one love' ethos nearly backfired one night when I ended up going to a club called The Gallery along with Bonehead and Johnno. What started as something innocent (which was really actually naiveté) took a dark turn, which went even darker for me.

We were in the club, which was a club that specialised in soul and funk; so naturally in the eighties most of the punters there were black. Now I'm colour blind when it comes to people, me, and so is Bonehead; but unfortunately not everyone out there shares our point of view. The world would be a far more peaceful place if they did, especially if they were necking all the pills that we were back then.

To us it was the Summer of Love and all we wanted was to share it and spread the word. We rocked up to the club; Bonehead was wide eyed and wearing a big white t-shirt and I was wearing a supersized psychedelic t-shirt. We'd popped some yellow New Yorker ecstasy tablets which in those days were top notch stuff, and we were loving the world. What we looked like to everyone in there, lord only knows.

We were instantly into the groove the moment we walked through the door, bouncing about to the music; and we obviously stood out like sore thumbs as none of us has any real dance moves. I'm just a big bloke with two left feet, but what I lacked in finesse I more than made up for in passion and loved to share. In our minds, we were the best dancers there were.

Before going in, and every few minutes once in there, Bonehead and Johnno kept warning me that under no circumstances should I ever go upstairs. As a big white bloke, it just wasn't done. Well, that just put the thought in my head. I was dancing away, all happy and loved up, and thinking about the futility of me not being able to go upstairs. We were all humans together, that's what I felt. Loving vibes all round, that was me.

Needless to say, within an hour of being in there, I was upstairs. There I was, prancing about on the ecstasy, sharing the love and talking to everyone; and I thought they were all buzzing off me. I mean, I was creating a ruckus in a place where you shouldn't create a ruckus, and I was saying things to certain people that you just should not say to certain people. In my head, it was all about spreading the love and everyone was in on it and loving me. In reality, I was causing hassle.

A big guy came up to me, put his arm around me and said, 'The exit's over there, mate,' whilst pointing with his free hand.

'The exit?' I responded, jigging about and sweating profusely. 'The exit is here,' pointing to my head, 'here,' to my heart, 'and here,' pointing everywhere, all profoundly, 'and I'm here.'

The guy who'd had his arm around me, in what I was now beginning to realise wasn't a friendly way, was obviously a bit of a big deal in the place. A big head, as we say in Manchester. Well, this big head wasn't too impressed with me, and proceeded to grab me and march me towards the exit.

Security noticed the commotion that was happening, and in all honesty, had probably been watching the tall white drugged up fool in the psychedelic t-shirt the entire duration I was there. They were probably ready to step in if it all went on top.

So, the bouncers stepped in and put me behind them, creating a human wall of security to protect me. Meanwhile the big head and his crew all wanted a piece of me and I didn't know where Bonehead and Johnno ended up, so things began to lose their lustre. That can happen with the happy drugs.

Alone, I decided to get out of there, and I left the club and all of the commotion that I'd managed to cause. The February cold air hit me hard and made my body shiver and react in the jagged way it can when on drugs. It was dark and it was quiet and all of a sudden, I was convinced that I could hear my car getting smashed up. It was pure paranoia kicking in and it wasn't going to be my friend. It wasn't my car, of course; and I couldn't honestly tell you whether a car was even being vandalised, but I doubt it.

Bonehead finally appeared, which momentarily gave me some mental ease. He had lost Johnno though, so we decided to grab a taxi.

Whichever way you slice it the whole situation had set me on a downward spiral, and I was officially 'going under'. The ecstasy had changed the chemistry in my head and turned into acid and a bad trip. For those of you reading this who are lucky enough to have never had a bad trip, I envy you. There is no logic, no rhyme or reason and your brain will tell you whatever it wants, normally triggered by surroundings, noise, and people around you, or your subconscious. Bad trips are hard to get out of once you're in them and are even worse when you have one on your own.

My brain was telling me at this point that my car was being smashed up, by people I'd pissed off, and logic (which wasn't there) would dictate that I was next. I decided I had to get out of there. I saw a taxi across the road, so we ran over to it. Bonehead fell into the front seat whilst I jumped in the back seat and laid down and told the driver where to take us in Withington. Without a word, the driver, cool as hell and looking like Bob Marley, began to drive.

I heard all of the doors lock at once, and my immediate thought was that we were trapped. Trying to stay calm, I focused on the music on the stereo. My mouth fell open when the album started playing. Who comes on? It was only New Order, *Technique*.

I said to the guy driving: 'Ere, mate, you're not into this are you?'

'I love this, man,' he responded. I was shocked and weirded out, as I knew these guys and knew Tony Wilson, and it was all too much of a coincidence for my twisted brain. It was a set up. That was my first illogical logical conclusion.

'You what? How can you? You know nothing about New Order! That album's only been out three days!' I shouted at him, or maybe I whispered. I don't know. 'How did you get hold of this?' I pushed on. I couldn't fathom how a cool-as-fuck black man could like my band, New Order, spawned of Joy Division. It just didn't sit right. It was silly, of course, as that's exactly what I'd been trying to do: bring my music to the masses. Here was proof music didn't conform to stereotypes, but my head wasn't in the place to deal with it.

I couldn't fathom it. It was before the days of internet leaks and downloads. Things weren't instant in those days. More to the point, I felt like New Order were mine. It seemed like a conspiracy, the doom only feeling increasingly oppressive as I decided he was taking me down all of the back roads and lanes to get to Withington; as if he was going to pull over any minute and dispose of me and Bonehead. New Order would be the soundtrack to our early deaths. That was what my chemically addled brain was telling me. I was all over the place in my illogical head.

'Just get us home, mate, please,' I pleaded.

'I'm getting you home, man. Chill,' he'd say each time.

As each track came on, I got more and more freaked out. As he stopped at each red light, I tried to get out but the child locks were on. He didn't know what I was going through, so every time I tugged on the door handle as we idled at a junction or lights, he thought I was trying to escape paying the fare. Meanwhile, the conspiracy against me was raging in my head. Anyone who hasn't taken chemicals, or has but has never had a bad experience, just wouldn't get what was happening to me. Be pleased about that. Once your mind sets itself down a dark path, it's very difficult to turn it round without a bit of time and nurturing, and/or the chemicals wearing off.

In the back seat of that cab, I was far from that. He finally drew to a halt in my street, and I was desperate to get out. I was showering him with gratitude and platitudes now, but I just wanted to get out of the car and into my house.

Shaking like a shitting dog, I paid the man and thanked him. He just grinned at me and drawled, 'Don't worry man, you're cool,' then high fived me.

Laughing nervously, I told him, 'You're too much, man. Seriously.'

Then he suddenly leaped forward at me, out of the car door window, shaking his dreads like they were a mane and shouting, 'I'M A LION, MAN!'

He roared at me and in my altered mind his head changed to what actually looked like a lion. I scarpered, shrieking like a child, with Bonehead following, shaking his head. Bonehead saw me safely through my front door and then vanished into the dark night.

I was living with my mum then, and walking into that kitchen was like I'd escaped hell. Fortunately, nobody was up, so I did what anyone in Britain would do. I made a cup of tea and put the TV on.

I'd taped *Top of the Pops* the previous night, so I thought that'd calm me down. I pressed play, and sat there with my tea, as the presenters introduced the first act:

'And now, in at number 22, it's New Order with "Round and Round".'

I put my tea down, turned off the TV, and went to bed to whimper under my covers.

Chapter Three
Spiked Island

When The Roses played Spike Island in May 1990, nobody was aware that it was a seminal moment. For us it was simply a way of progressing our beautiful city and our beautiful music.

It's a gig that will go down in history, and was famous for having bad sound through technical issues and the wind blowing the sound about; and there wasn't enough beer and it ran out almost as soon as it all started; and then there were the security guards that were bastards to anyone trying to get in or out of the whole affair.

Yet Spike Island, the huge, chaotic Stone Roses gig on a reclaimed toxic waste site in Cheshire, will always be remembered as a key moment in British pop culture, when the Madchester scene broke out into the open and one of the best British indie bands of all time had their moment in the sun – or, at least, the outdoors. I mean, this *was* up north, after all. As it turned out the sun did actually shine, along with the sound-ruining wind.

No one really anticipated how big it was going to be. In the end, over 28,000 people turned up to watch hour upon hour of support bands, all leading up to the Roses. It was huge. And it was nearly all kids, many younger than us at that time.

Keen to be part of history, despite not having tickets, we concocted a plan to drive down there the night before the gig in Bonehead's van. There was me, of course Bonehead, John Morrin and numerous others including Chris Hutton. Bizarrely, I was to meet other future members of Oasis who were all there in different groups.

Ensuring we had a decent enough supply of narcotics, we did some picking of magic mushrooms so that we had something recreational to make the time go by while we waited for the Mancunian musical mammoths that were the Roses.

We also took other things. Up, down, sideways. We were there to party and we intended to take what helped us do exactly that.

Keeping to the plan to go to the area the day before the big gig, we all bundled into Bonehead's van and trundled our way to Spike Island. The gig itself was to be in a part of the island that were essentially isolated fields near Widnes. It wasn't exactly an area of beauty, being filled with stunted trees, giant pylons and a dodgy looking green little lake type things. Nearby was the ICI chemical works, just to add to the stunning view. We drove about looking for somewhere that was near that beauty spot so that we could hole up waiting for the big day. We were all full of excitement and those good nerves you get before something massive and positive happens.

It had been all over the press, and anyone into their music was buzzing about The Stone Roses. Whether they were in Manchester or not, this was something everyone wanted a slice of. And we were there!

So, after scooting round in a van so garish it could be seen from space, we came across a field near to where you got into Spike Island, and we drove onto it to settle down and wait. We also intended to hide from any farmers, of course. Or at least that's what we thought we had to do. Now, if you don't already know what Bonehead's van looked like, then you won't realise how conspicuous it was. It didn't blend in. Not anywhere.

Imagine if Jackson Pollock was given a Mazda 1800 pick-up truck and free licence to do with it what he wanted. Then take away some of the talent, add a few bottles of wine to the artistic process, and you'll have an idea of what Bonehead's automobile looked like. It stuck out like a sore thumb. So of course, before you know it, the farmer whose field it was rocked up and surprisingly said, 'Lads, I don't mind you staying here for the night, but to stop anyone else, I'm locking that gate now and won't be opening it until 10am.'

Spot on, we thought. We had our own private field, and we were happy as pigs in shite, to use a colloquial term.

As darkness fell, we built a camp fire and thought we'd have a party of it, as you do. We were young, foolish and didn't care, and we had a load of drugs with us. So we dropped some Es, did some whizz and got down to be all outdoorsy. Next thing you know, we heard some unmistakable drum beats and guitar and realised that we could hear the Stone Roses doing a sound check.

Well, you can imagine what we were like! We were ecstatic, and it wasn't just the ecstasy that was coursing through our collective veins. That said, I'm sure it helped. We all got up, dancing away and feeling like we were the only ones in the world listening to it. It was magical.

Anyway, we listened to the Stone Roses do their sound check and had a great time of it, feeling on top of the world with our sneak preview. After a while, and way after our impromptu sneak preview had finished, we began to get more mellow and then finally everyone tried to kip down in the back of the van. It's at this stage that I have to piece together the rest of what happened then and the next day, as I fear I may have over indulged in substances that have a wayward effect on the parts of the brain that do all of the mental filing. A lot of what follows is what I've been reliably told.

I'm told at around 3am the morning of Spike Island, I decided it would be the height of fun to reverse the van to the other side of the field. This was with everyone sleeping in the back, including Bonehead. I snuck into the driver's seat like a ninja, doing my best not to disturb any of the lads in the back.

I turned the key, crunched it into reverse gear immediately and floored the accelerator!

So, there I was, hurtling in reverse as fast as the van would go, revs screaming, and swerving all over the farmer's field. I thought it was funny as fuck! Someone in the back opened one of the rear doors and people began falling out of the back, left right and centre, in the pitch dark in the middle of a field.

Bonehead was always one of those people that rarely lost his temper, but when he did, he went ballistic. He roared at me to stop what I was doing and made me turn off the engine and hand him back the keys. As I did, the silence of pre-dawn Cheshire was occasionally broken by the groans and swearing of those that my prank had unceremoniously ejected from the van and potentially onto shitpiles in the field.

Needless to say, Bonehead wasn't best pleased and lost the plot with me. He launched himself at me when I climbed back out of the van, me still thinking everything was hilarious until he connected with me horizontally. We rolled and grappled with each other, but it didn't really come to very much. He's only little anyway and compared to my big frame he didn't really stand a chance physically. It ended up being more about swearing than actual punching or kicking, but he was pissed off, I can tell you that.

It fizzled out quickly but not without more harsh words and a cloud of sulk over us. So, with differences mostly put to one side and daylight arriving after very little sleep thanks to my shenanigans, it was the day that Stone Roses played and made some history.

I've spent years puzzling over one thing about this day. No matter how you approach it, you have to cross a bridge to get over on to Spike Island. For over three decades I haven't been able to work it out, I honestly haven't. I watched the recent film, and it had me puzzling over so many aspects, as it was all a blur to me.

I've even got a picture of a load of us stood by McGuigan, Bonehead, Chris Johnson, and Chris Hutton, all in our individual gangs, and some of us are stood on top of that crazy van. We'd all come separately, none of them knew each other and yet there they all stood around me. I knew all of them individually, and so I was the common denominator there.

It wasn't until I watched a video of the actual event containing footage that no one else has seen that things finally began to click into place. The blur was taken away slightly, and I realised that the reason that I couldn't remember a bridge was because I didn't go over a bloody bridge! I didn't have a ticket, you see. So, me and a friend called Ricky Heffernan went alongside the river, and we saw that some other resourceful scallywags had made a kind of raft to get in on.

Well, that all seemed like lot of bother, so not being arsed with that, we then went in like the SAS and under the radar. We found ourselves a big log that we held on to and made our way there by floating along on the water. We were fully clothed but didn't give a shit. How we didn't lose it and drown I do not know, but we made it.

We dried off and met up with everyone and had an absolute blast. Well, so I'm told anyway. Apart from the van picture, there isn't much evidence to remind me of what went on.

I'd seen the Roses before a year or so earlier, and it was a very different type of gig. They were playing Warrington, the same place they recently returned to for their film *Made of Stone*.

There was me, and John the Duck, who was later to tour manage the Roses as well as become Ian Brown's personal assistant. We all bundled into whatever car I had at the time and set off happy as Larry McMullen on our way to Warrington.

On the way there, we hit some fog that was a proper pea souper. We tried and tried to get through it but ended up having to stop on the top of what we assumed was a hill. We only knew it was a hill as while we couldn't see anything through the windscreen, we could definitely tell we were climbing. Just climbing really slowly. It didn't help that we'd all had the biggest spliff on the way and were stoned as bastards.

Well, there we were, stranded and unable to see a few feet ahead of us. The headlights just seemed to hit a white wall and we didn't really know what to do. We got out of the car, and I started to put the fear into the others by saying it was like a scene from *American Werewolf in London*. Howls ensued and I was told to shut up, but it only made me do it more.

Before long, either the real fog cleared, or our cannabis fog cleared in our heads, and we were able to face driving onwards to the gig. It was only my second one, so I was adamant I was going to get there.

And get there we did. We swaggered in to see them in full swing up on stage, looking cool as fuck and smashing it to the much smaller crowd than they were to play to later at Spike Island.

It was awesome. We got on it, danced through the crowd and were having it down the front of the stage without a care in the world. John the Duck was gesturing to them as we danced there. It was his first bit of recognition and he was loving it, so when he gets too full of himself, I always have to remind him of what happened later that night.

Well, needless to say, the Roses smashed it. They tore the roof down. We all met up with the lads backstage and then decided that we didn't want the party to end, so headed off to The Hacienda to carry on the festivities.

We rocked up, full of beans and ready to tear it apart. Dancing away, high on life and all other things, we spotted Bernard Sumner, who had transitioned from Joy Division to New Order.

Now little John is a right character, a proper lovable little rogue. He was mates with the Roses and was well in with the Happy Mondays, even popping up in their 'Lazyitis' video, and it turned out that he'd begun to become known by New Order; specifically, Bernard.

He bounded up to him and they got to talking. I sloped off, either to go to the toilets or the bar or both and left them to it. A few minutes later, I came back, and John the Duck was sat with Bernard making him roar laughing.

As I said, he became the tour manager for the Roses later and was again on their recent return. He also is Ian Brown's PA. I see him regularly in Manchester, and we always have stories to reminisce about over a coffee; he's from the top drawer is John.

I'm also a mate of Mani from the Roses as well. He's the soundest, loveliest man, who always looks after his own, just like Ian Brown, who I met at a house belonging to a friend called Iggy. I asked him why his flares were shredded and torn at the bottom.

'Perpetual motion,' came the reply.

As cool as they come.

Chapter Four
Pretty Clean

After Strangeways and the Spike Island event I had a good long look at myself in the mirror (taken under advice). I came to a very important decision. In order for me to progress in life I had two options. The first and most elusive option was to be involved in the music industry. It was what lit my fire. The second and more realistic option would be to knuckle down and get a nine to five. After all, that's what all my friends were doing. But I knew that just wouldn't do. So, I looked at my strengths. I had always got on well with people and I was shrewd financially. Only one option really. Build a business empire. Well, sort of.

Over the next few days I read all the local papers looking for an opportunity that read 'big-time'. Instead I got local window cleaning rounds and Tupperware parties. Not really my scene. Then a stroke of good fortune came a-knocking. I was mulling over my prospects, enjoying a pint in The Packhorse on Stockport Road, Levenshulme, when I spotted an old pal called Jason Watson.

After a couple of glasses, a very prosperous and healthy-looking Jason spilled his secret. He had started a car valeting firm and was doing very well for himself. Not only that, he was also offering me an opportunity to come on board and learn the ropes. Never the man to argue with fate, I wholeheartedly agreed, and so a new adventure began.

Bright and sharp the next morning I was outside Jason's house. Over the next few weeks I would help Jason valet his clients' vehicles. His clients were mainly based in the affluent county of Cheshire, as Jason had quite rightly figured there was more expendable cash in this area. It wasn't long before I was into the books, how much the operation cost to run, the little tricks of the trade, and to be honest I was loving every minute of it.

With encouragement from Jason, both motivationally and financially, Formula One Valeting was born. I will never forget the feeling of standing next to my first ever Transit van. I know that might sound a little underwhelming to some but to me it was everything.

So, I started small. Not much choice really. I think the fact that it was my own business really drove me on in the beginning. I had never been offered a chance before and I was determined not to waste it.

I worked long days and short nights, rain (mostly) or shine (literally) and it all soon caught up with me. After a month I was physically exhausted. Obviously, I had to work smarter not harder before I found myself six foot under. I decided that I needed firstly, a second pair of hands, and secondly, a first class marketing campaign. I scoured the local talent pool for suitable valeters. I was looking for a young man who was eager to learn and could hold a cloth in his hand and his tongue in his head.

When it came to marketing, my training with Jason was put to good use. Just as he had done, I spent considerable time looking for a new angle on the market. Jason had picked an area that was cash rich. That made the difference. I decided to pick an industry that was cash rich instead. And one that was very close to my heart. Football. And boy, did that make a difference.

I set out devising a plan to install myself as the valeter for my own team, Manchester United. Well, why not? Start at the top I say. So, after much scratching of head I decided to use probably my greatest tool. Front. But for that I would need an opportunity, a window. Whilst still unsure of how to manufacture this, I cracked on with my recruitment drive.

On a cold November evening I decided to pay a visit to my mate Steve Shenton. Steve was a friend from West Point who was a stand-up fella with a quick wit and a winning personality. I was hoping he might want to help me out valeting, which was a long shot, but worth a go. The long shot was exactly that and after a no-no from Steve I was ready to leave.

Suddenly I heard a right commotion coming from the room next door. Steve laughed and opened the door to the room. Inside stood Mark, Steve's younger brother, surrounded by a few of his friends. One lad in particular seemed to be the cause of the commotion. He was laughing loudly whilst hurling insults at his mates around a small snooker table. It seemed he had been caught cheating but was vigorously defending himself by attacking others verbally.

'Keep it down dickheads,' shouted Steve.

'Shut it you, you're nothing to do with this,' laughed back the kid.

I admired the gall of the young fella. He was a few years younger than Steve but that didn't seem to bother him. I decided to join in.

'What's your name?' I asked.

'You the police?' he fired back.

'Ha, no I'm not. I'm Paul Ashbee.'

This stopped the kid. He pondered for a moment.

'I think you know my brothers.'

'Who are?'

'Paul and Noel.'

It suddenly all made sense. I did know both his brothers. One of them was a larger than life, good humoured, outspoken character whilst the other was a bit more subdued but with a rapier-like wit. It seemed the younger brother had both the confidence and the wit.

'Are you working kid? Do you want a job?' I asked. The kid had something personable about him; he was a likeable fella.

'Depends on what it is and how much you'll pay me mate.'

So, a few minutes later, with a job description provided and a rate of pay agreed, I had my new employee.

Suddenly realising, I laughed, 'I don't even know your name, mate.'

The boy laughed along, his large kid-like eyes sparkling beneath his thick dark eyebrows. He extended his hand.

'Liam, mate. Liam Gallagher.'

The following morning, at six am, I'm tooting my horn outside a house on a cul-de-sac on a Burnage estate. The front door opens and my new recruit, Liam, bounds out enthusiastically.

'Morning Boss,' he greets me as he hops into the front seat of the Transit, knocking empty crisp packets and drink cartons off his seat.

'Morning. Don't ever call me boss again.'

'Won't do, Boss.' He laughs.

And so began my relationship with Liam John Paul Gallagher. Liam was an extremely hard worker and learned quickly over the next few days. We were mainly cleaning cars around the city centre of Manchester and then a few over Alderley Edge way.

Liam was always positive and the clients he came into contact with seemed to be left with a good impression. A name he would receive later in his life would be 'Liams' as he had many different facets to his personality although at this early stage it was less evident.

We would discuss music a lot, or rather Liam would pester me to regale him with tales of the bands I'd been to see. We talked and listened to The Roses, New Order, Echo and the Bunnymen, A Certain Ratio, The Mondays. Liam became engrossed in it all. He also became a vital part of the business and over the next few months I grew very fond of the cheeky yet lovable teenager who always had an answer and a smile whatever the situation.

So, with my resource issues now resolved it was time to move onto the next part of my plan and secure that contract with Manchester United. To complete such I had devised a cunning plan that involved an innocent and gullible Liam Gallagher. It would take a while to happen though.

Progressing and promoting the business had begun to take all my attention, although I always had time for a drink and a chat with Bonehead.

'Starting a band,' he announced mid-pint one evening. He continued to tell me about a young Levenshulme fella he had met called Guigsy. It seemed that Bonehead's love of musicianship had been matched by Guigsy's and the enthusiasm was flashing across his face.

'Guess I'll be up front then?' I teased.

'Nope, we've got Chris Huts up front and Tony McCarroll on drums,' he beamed triumphantly. 'We've called ourselves The Rain.'

I knew both Tony and Chris from the park. Although I wouldn't say I knew them well, I knew enough to know they were good fellas. I didn't know they were into music though.

'Have you rehearsed yet?' I asked.

'Rehearsed? We've already played a gig.'

Jesus, things move fast around here, I thought, and if I'm honest I felt a little bit of regret in not chasing down my musical aspirations. Bonehead went on to tell me that they were playing Times Square in Didsbury the following Thursday.

I'd often talk of Bonehead to Liam and when I mentioned going to watch his new band, he was extremely eager. He already knew Tony the drummer but wasn't aware he had joined a band.

The following Thursday we were there early. Why I'm not sure, as the availability of expendable cash was somewhat limited. As we entered, I spotted Tony McCarroll at the bar and he bought us both a drink. The night was off to a flyer. Liam and Tony caught up as the place slowly filled and Tony vanished backstage.

After a 30-minute set I was suitably impressed. Bonehead was obviously the driving force in the band as I knew he would be. They sang a song about Strangeways which Bonehead had written after his visits to see me. It was a good song and I could see that Liam was engrossed by it all.

Liam was looking forward to meeting Bonehead after hearing so many hilarious stories about him. Unfortunately, due to a misunderstanding regarding the true owner of the two drinks we were hurriedly slurping, an argument ensued, and we had to leave early. Shame really, but the next meeting between Bonehead and Liam would prove a lot more fateful.

Me and Liam cracked on for the next six months in the glamorous world of valeting. I was still working on getting the United contract, but to no avail.

Over this period, I came to realise that young Liam was one confused kid. At times he acted like he was Pacino in *Scarface*, like he owned the world. He would cause a ruction through his verbal attacks and aggressive put-downs and then he would become almost shy and demure, like a polite public schoolboy.

People often thought that the relationship between Liam and me was an unusual one. I suppose it was if you consider the difference in age and the fact that he had older brothers already, but neither of us really thought it at the time.

That's where I fitted in though: Liam was at a stage in his life when he needed a brotherly figure, or a male that looked after him. So, there you go, a few people thought and commented on the fact that me and Liam was an odd relationship. But you know what? I'm a true believer that we're all here for a reason, whatever that reason is. And it's all about what you make of it. You know what I mean?

Chapter Five
Life on the Cliff

I'm sat in the van with Liam one wet, windy and altogether miserable Wednesday morning. The mood is low. The valeting business, after a terrific start, is beginning to take a bit of a dip, and for the first time we find ourselves without work.

'What are we going to do?' asked Liam despondently.

'Don't worry Will, I've got a plan,' I lied.

Well, sort of lied. I did have a plan. It was the same plan I'd had for the previous twelve months but had taken no action on. Authorised valeter for Manchester United PLC.

'I'm waiting for the right opportunity my mate, to approach United.'

'Fuck United, get your arse down to City,' Liam came back.

Liam was a vociferous and match-going City fan. We would spend hours lobbing football banter about or hurling insults, criticisms and downright lies at each other. It was always in good spirit, mind.

'Thanks for the direction Liam. Have you ever thought of becoming a motivational speaker?' I teased.

'I could if I wanted to,' fired back Liam. An aspect of Liam's character that was slightly flawed was the chasm between what he said he would do and what he actually had the confidence to complete. I would often call him out on it, which led to some heated conversations.

'Yeah, well, why don't you?'

'Cos, I don't want to.' I could forget just how young Liam was at times but answers like this reminded me.

'What do you want to do then?'

'I want to front the biggest band in the world,' came his ridiculous reply.

Three days later I'm sat with Bonehead in the Milestone Pub on Burnage Lane. He is unusually pensive and serious.

'Might be the end of the band: we've had to let Chris go,' he revealed. It seemed that after the initial rush and a handful of gigs The Rain had decided there was no way forward for them as a band, and if I'm honest I never really thought that Chris was the right man for them. Never one to miss out on an opportunity I piped up.

'I've a friend who has a voice like an angel, the looks of a fucking rock star and the presence to front any band on this planet,' I exaggerated. I'd never actually heard Liam sing and was totally unsure as to how he would react in front of a crowd, but nevertheless…

'Who is it?' asked a suddenly interested Bonehead.

'Liam. Liam Gallagher,' I replied. 'Do you want me to get him to audition for you?'

'Shit, why not, who is he?' And with the clink of two glass pint pots the future of British rock for the next two decades or so was sorted. Now all I had to do was convince Liam that he had the ability to sing and the confidence to get on a stage.

The following Monday I'm outside Liam's house on Cranbourne Drive, Burnage. As usual, he energetically leaps into the van, mouth running off.

'I've got some good news for you,' I said, which silenced him.

'Have you? What is it? A pay rise?'

'Have you been sniffing glue? A fucking pay rise? Jesus. No, I've got you an audition to front Bonehead's band.'

The wave of joy and excitement that I was expecting did not materialise. Instead, facing me was a suddenly pale and stammering young man.

'You've got me what? An audition? Why the fuck have you done that?'

As I explained earlier Liam's bravado was most of the time just that.

'What the fuck's up with you? You said you wanted to do it,' I cajoled, but to no avail. I spent the rest of the day cleaning four Transit vans with a very subdued and almost silent Liam.

On the way home I broached the subject again.

'So, when do you want to do it?'

'Do what?'

'Audition for the band.'

'I don't,' came a very certain reply, and with that Liam hopped out of the van and up the front path to his door.

Over the next fortnight I would daily tease Liam about his lack of confidence and he would tell me to fuck right off. I asked him to sing for me and he told me to fuck right off. I asked him to try and write some lyrics and again he told me to fuck right off. I was using the dripping tap method to influence and encourage him. Finally, one afternoon, mid valet, Liam turned to me and mumbled: 'Tell your mate Bonehead I'll come around this weekend if he wants.'

'Fuckin ace fella,' I replied enthusiastically, and immediately made a plan to go and see Bonehead after work to organise. I never even found out what changed his mind because to be honest, I didn't care. I was just elated that he had.

The weekend after, I and one nervous looking Liam Gallagher headed over to Fallowfield to visit Bonehead and his missus Kate. I rapped on his front door and was greeted by Bone, who welcomed both me and Liam inside. After handshakes and introductions Liam suddenly let out a shriek. Bonehead had been holding a dead tarantula spider in his hand and had thrown it at Liam. One way to break the ice, I guess.

And so, it began. Bonehead pulled out an acoustic guitar and after much shuffling of feet and nervous twitching Liam opened his mouth and began to sing. I looked at Bonehead, who smiled and gave me an approving nod.

Soon after, myself, Liam and Bonehead drove over to Gorton to visit Tony, the drummer. No introductions were required this time around as Tony already knew Liam and within minutes Liam was singing again, with Bonehead strumming and Tony on the bongos. Once again everybody seemed as pleased as Punch.

I left Bonehead at Tony's as me and Liam headed back to Burnage.

'What did you think?' he enquired cautiously.

'You were made for it Liam, can you not see that?' I replied. Although Liam exuded confidence I was always very careful to encourage and praise him as I knew most of his confidence was for show.

'Really?' he beamed.

'Yes, really,' I confirmed.

A smile as wide as the Manchester Ship Canal spread across his face and he playfully punched me. This was his time, his moment and I really hoped it would pay off for him.

In the meantime though it was back to reality with the valeting business. With the downturn in demand over and the business back on the positive I decided we needed to recruit someone to work with Liam.

I put the feelers out with the normal suspects including Bonehead and the next morning not only did I have Liam in the van but also Tony McCarroll.

Tony had just finished a job in construction and was looking for something to fill the gap before his next contract started, so everybody was happy.

Each morning now began with the dreams and aspirations of two budding musicians, which immediately rubbed off on my good self. If these two fellas could chase their dreams down then why couldn't I? And with that thought came a moment of inspiration, and a crackpot idea that was to change my life.

Two days later I implemented my cunning and brilliant plan. I had a client in Alderley Edge who I occasionally looked after. On a previous visit he had pointed out that his next door neighbour was none other than the Welsh and Manchester United striker Mark Hughes.

After finishing his car I handed Liam an envelope and asked him to deliver it next door. I told him it was an invoice but instead it was a message that read 'Curly, I think I love you.' I was hoping the tightly permed and sometime fiery and aggressive Mark Hughes had a sense of humour. If not, Liam was a fast runner. To facilitate his escape, and also watch the proceedings, I pulled the van up at the bottom of Hughesy's driveway.

I started to peal with laughter the minute Mark Hughes opened the door. Tony was looking at me bewildered, which seemed to make it even funnier. Liam handed the note over and Mark Hughes read it. I was now howling, as I saw Hughesy laughing, so I hopped out the van. Liam was pulling a face as he realised he'd been had but I needed to grasp my opportunity.

'Hiya Mark, the name's Bigun…' Ten minutes later, after a lengthy and entertaining conversation, I was sauntering down his driveway awaiting a phone call regarding the position of the official car valeter for Manchester United Football Club.

It would take a month or two to come to fruition and during this time I guess more focus than ever was on the band. One immediate change that Liam brought about was a new name.

We were sat in his bedroom one evening with Chris Johnson and David Coates. There was a massive poster on the wall that advertised an Inspiral Carpets tour that was happening in 1991. One of the venues being promoted was a gaff in Swindon called the Oasis. We were all lobbing names in: I remember The Braemars, Lollipop and The Hugo's when Chris pointed at the Inspiral Carpets poster and announced the name 'Oasis'. After a very short discussion it was agreed. Oasis was the new name for the band. Small moments in time like these always bring a smile to my face. All these years later and that name has been uttered in every far-flung corner of this planet by countless people.

Oasis was born.

Me and Liam had decided to visit Didsbury library in search of lyrics. I had read one of The Mondays in an interview citing it as a great place for lyrical inspiration.

I roared as I read a Bible I had picked up.

'It's like reading the lyrics for a Stone Roses album,' I laughed, to hisses and shushes all round.

Liam snatched the Bible from me and laughed as well. We visited a number of times and from these visits and with Bonehead's musical accompaniment the songs 'Life in Vain', 'Take Me', 'Reminisce' and 'She Always Comes Up Smiling' were born.

Rehearsals had upped and even Tony agreed that Liam was a fresh change that had been needed. Tony had been upset when Chris Hutton had been ousted from the band but luckily for all he was already a friend of Liam's.

The band were really beginning to tighten, and you could hear the wall of sound that the rhythm section would bring to early Oasis beginning to blossom. You could also see the confidence growing in Liam daily. At this stage he had a more angelic tone to his vocal rather than the rasping snarl he produces nowadays. More of that later.

The car valeting business began to become flexible around the band's needs and we would often finish early if Bone and Guigs were available. We were rehearsing in a number of places including the Grove in Longsight. After one evening spent raiding the bar there and then being booted out because the band was smoking the herb, I returned home in a pretty sombre mood. My father handed me a rumpled scrap of paper with a name and number scrawled across it. My eyes widened as I read the name - 'Mark Yewes'. My dad was never very good at spelling but that was ignored as I desperately ran to the hall to make the call.

'Hiya, Mark, it's Bigun, I mean Paul, you know the valeter,' I stammered, reminding myself to calm down and behave sober.

'They're gonna give you a trial week down at the Cliff. You can clean mine first.'

'You're the best fuckin Welshman that I know, and your car is on the house my friend. I won't let you down, I promise.'

As always with words they were delivered with the best of intentions but without any knowledge whatsoever of what the future might bring. Well, that's the way I deal with what then fucking happened.

The following week me, Tony and Liam were sat in the shiniest white van in England outside the gates of the Cliff training ground, home of Manchester United FC. The Cliff was formerly the home of Broughton Rugby Club and stood on the banks of the River Irwell. It hosted rugby until 1933 whereafter United took over things.

I was looking at the gates and I was in a bit of a state. I was fucking bursting with pride at finally getting to work for the club I'd adored since I was a kid, but also acutely aware that this was only a trial week and one that I was more than capable of fucking up. I wanted to celebrate rather than concentrate, which wasn't good.

'Right boys, this is really important,' I began.

'Ha. Look at you, you're pale fucking white,' laughed Liam, as Tony joined in.

'Seriously, don't fuck it up,' I pleaded, but was only met with more wails of laughter. I decided to leave it and act nonchalant in a desperate act of reverse psychology, which luckily worked.

Thirty minutes later we were greeted by Mark Hughes, who introduced us to security and pointed at where we could set our equipment up. We did just that and then we were off, as player after player pulled up and threw their car keys at us. Schmeichel, Giggsy, Pallister, Bruce, Kanchelskis, Robbo, Ince and the rest. I was loving it - these are my idols - but I was wise enough to play it down.

We were mainly cleaning Mercedes and Beemers as there wasn't much demand for the supercar even though they were certainly super cars to us. I have to credit Liam and Tony, the first few months down there we cleaned every car to within an inch of its primer. We were polite and efficient and would help out with other maintenance stuff around the place. It wasn't long before we were helping out with personal affairs and generally having a good giggle. We became part of one big family whilst there, unknowing that great things were about to explode within both the football club and the band.

At first, meeting Fergie on a daily basis was daunting. He is a fiery man, as many have described before, but I soon cottoned on to the fact that if I talked about horse racing he would become sociable, almost friendly even. I would often see tips written down in his car although whenever I checked up on them afterwards they always seemed to have lost.

It was probably the most beautiful period of my life, even to this day. On a daily basis we would all work hard, but we would bounce off all the different personalities in the place. It's like the old saying: 'If you enjoy what you do, you'll never work another day in your life.' And that's how it felt.

On top of this things were progressing rapidly with the band. We had organised a gig at the Boardwalk in Manchester. It was to be the first time that Oasis were to appear and so it was a big deal to us. On top of that Bonehead had arranged some recording time for us, on the premise that he would plaster the actual studio that we would use, and we would have to help out through labouring. It was an unusual arrangement but one that worked for all.

So, it was August 1991, and Oasis made their debut appearance at the Boardwalk, Manchester. The club would soon become home to the band as a rehearsal spot, but first they would entertain the patrons upstairs. Only they didn't. The three songs in the set all had 'performance issues' so we ended up playing six songs. Or rather, the same three set song, twice. This was followed by a splattering of applause solely from those who were with the band.

It was strange. I had watched them rehearse for the previous year and knew that Liam's stage presence was their strongest asset. Yet on that first night, it just wasn't there. He hid behind the microphone rather than swaggering in front of it. He took to staring and talking to Tony as he banged away on his kit. How he imagined Tony could hear him I don't know.

Although I wasn't impressed, the people I was watching with certainly were. I was with a small crowd from Levenshulme. Stood next to me was Noel, Liam's brother. He quite rightly picked up on the performance issues but he was certainly excited by what he had seen.

'They've got something. Fuck knows what that something is but they've got it.' I knew his opinion would be important to Liam and I was very pleased it was so positive.

Anyway, it was general deflation in the dressing room afterwards. I tried to ease the tension. 'Boys, it's your first fucking performance together, there was always going to be problems. Your Noel fuckin loved it Liam.'

There was a general murmur of agreement and within moments we were back on track, ready to go again. To prove such I arranged for a return gig at The Boardwalk at the start of 1992. This would give the lads another four months or so to rehearse and write, which could only be a good thing.

Rehearsals mainly consisted of long jamming sessions interspersed with smoke and tea breaks. It was in such a session that Noel was first mentioned as a potential band member, which I guess was an obvious leap but one which was fraught with potential pitfalls. We decided to sleep on it.

Chapter 6
And Four Becomes Five

I first met Noel Gallagher in the early eighties. He was a quiet lad with a quick reply if required. He dressed well and mainly hung around with Vinnie Young and Chris Johnson from Burnage.

Although the three of them lived in Burnage most of their time was spent in Levenshulme with the likes of Howsey and Panda on Greenbank or in Errwood Park. They had quite a tidy City away firm and I guess that's where I first met Noel. I liked Noel as I thought him intelligent and funny. Although he was never the loudest in the group, if he had something to say, it got said.

I would also bump into him at various gigs around the place. One place he frequented regularly was the Thunderdome on Rochdale Road, on the outskirts of the city centre. This was probably the first underground dance club in Manchester and was filled by the most energetic and unpredictable crowd you could imagine.

Although I never knew the connection, Noel would often be with Mani from The Roses at these events, so he was always respected amongst the locals, including me. I guess we had always got on due to our mutual love of the Mancunian holy trinity – football, music and clobber.

When the boys first suggested that Noel join Oasis, I was slightly wary. I was happy with the group dynamic and thought that another personality might upset such. It had also become very apparent that Liam looked towards Noel as a guiding figure as you would with most big brothers. The problem lay in the fact that Noel didn't look at it in the same way. For instance, after his excitement at The Boardwalk gig he had then told Liam that his band was 'shite'. This did not do much for the young fella's ego I can tell you.

They were strange times, the eighties. We were all tight as friends, but we never did each other favours if you know what I mean. There certainly wasn't anything such as a bromance and if you didn't get arrested or beaten up you would point and laugh at those that did.

They were harsh and tough times and you had to be able to handle yourself both physically and verbally. This tough exterior certainly applied to Noel and in no circumstance more strongly than with his youngest brother. I felt that it might lead to problems further down the line which turned out to be a prophecy that turned into a policy.

On the other hand, I knew that Noel had many connections within the music industry that could possibly propel us to superstardom, so after much debate and thought I decided that Noel joining was a positive.

I spoke to Bonehead, who had only heard of Noel through Liam, and reassured him that it was a good move. For the last twelve months each member of the band had found their position. Bonehead's was definitely that of musical director. All the creativity, structure and organisation came from him and I suppose asking another songwriter on board would affect him more than most.

But as usual Bonehead laughed any rivalry off.

'It can only be a good thing; besides, he's promising free guitar strings that he's gonna pinch from The Inspiral Carpets,' he giggled.

And so Oasis became a five-piece band.

To be honest there wasn't the initial progression we were all expecting. Noel was still on tour with the Inspiral Carpets, so infrequently attended rehearsals. Noel did bring a song with him though, called 'I Better Let You Know'. The band worked on it and everything fitted into place so the song was added to the set. This was Noel's only musical offering after his arrival and I worried about the number of songs that we had managed to put together.

One evening we were in our new rehearsal room. The Inspiral Carpets had been rehearsing in The Boardwalk and so Noel had become aware of a rehearsal space up for grabs which we duly grabbed.

There had been a long jam that night on a new song which had been labelled 'Columbia'. This was due to Noel naming the South American country as his favourite place in the world to visit, and I don't think it was the scenery he appreciated. After we had finished Noel announced that he had some news. The band would be appearing on national television! There were whoops and hollers and excited questions.

The mood quickly fizzled away when Noel announced we were going on to Comic Relief in support of Alvin Stardust at Granada Studios. For the next twenty minutes we took the piss out of Noel for organising such a shit gig but really we were all secretly excited at the chance of appearing on the box.

On the day we all in hopped into Bonehead's van and made our way to Granada Studios Tour site, which was located at the arse end of Manchester city centre. Upon arrival we made our way to the dressing room, where Alvin Stardust awaited with his shiny white teeth, pitch black hair and massive pointed leather shoulders. I pointed and started to roar laughing but Noel hushed me and gave me one of his looks. I decided I was best not present so me and a couple of others went for a mooch (look around). A couple of fire exit doors later I was marching down the cobbles of Coronation Street, or at least the set on which it was filmed. This was the beginning of something new, and we were all in high spirits as I heard a crack and the door to the Kabin newsagents was suddenly wide open. With a roar of laughter my two compatriots were inside, and were seriously talking about robbing the place. I stood in amazement as they headed immediately for the cigarettes behind the counter and started stuffing them in various pockets. I followed this by falling around in laughter as they tail-arsed out of the place, panicked looks on their faces, and headed back towards the van.

Just to make sure I checked one of the cigarette packs and, as expected, it was as empty as my friends' heads. Like everything else in the shop, or the street, the cigarette boxes were merely props.

When I returned Liam and the band were ready to go. They fired out 'Take Me' on Alvin Stardust's musical equipment to a small crowd and it went down well. Not well enough to be actually broadcast though, which pissed everybody off.

On the way out we were accosted by security, who had discovered empty cigarette packets littered all down Coronation Street. We pleaded our innocence, which we were extremely experienced at, and soon security calmed down and let us on our way. I remember getting a withering look from Noel though.

Following this it was back to rehearsals and talk of another gig. This one was at Dartford Polytechnic and again was organised by Noel. Noel had definitely become more active in his role and I guessed we hoped it would be the start of a worldwide tour. I mean, it was every boy's dream come true. Touring the country and hopefully the world as roadies with your mates for a band that also consisted of your mates! What could go fucking wrong?

So, we rolled up at Dartford, bristling with Mancunian street attitude and a thirst for everything. We are expecting a few naive students in what we considered to be a one-horse town. When we arrived it was like fucking Millwall were waiting for us. As we passed in the minibus there was a confused look on Noel's face. Rather than the intellectual student gathering we were expecting the polytechnic to provide, there seemed to be a hundred-strong mob of aggressive males instead.

'Maybe they're not here for us?' Noel said hopefully.

But he was wrong. As soon as the band walked on that stage there was an air of menace about the place. The more aggressive had moved to the front of the hall, which was not good. The problem here was Liam. Now in every other band I've seen, the lead singer very rarely gets taunted the way Liam does. And it began early, long before any notoriety in the press.

They started gobbing off to Liam, who in typical fashion was wearing none of it.

'You what you prick? I'll loosen your fucking teeth in a minute,' he snarled at some gooner giving it out in the crowd.

Working for the United Nations had never been an option for Liam Gallagher. His words were visibly riling the crowd and we were readying ourselves for a full-on battle when the music finally began and drowned out whatever vulgarities were being hurled towards and from the stage. There were at least six of us there and we all knew how to handle ourselves.

I stayed to watch the gig as the rest of the group sidled off. The performance was good and I was really impressed with how professional the boys were now sounding. Liam's presence really was his strength and the more aggressive he was the more the crowd seemed to lap it up. At the end of the performance I was backstage in the dressing room. The mood was one of exuberance; Liam was recalling what he had said to his aggressors in the crowd and Noel was just happy with the performance. The mood quickly dampened though when the promoter arrived.

'We don't have the money to pay you,' he for some reason gleefully announced.

There was an almost comedic intake of breath by all before Liam started to boot off.

'What do you fuckin mean, there's no money to pay us? Do you want fucking filling in? Why the fuck are you happy about it?'

Liam was now furious and rightly so. We had paid nearly 200 quid for a van and fuel and now this nugget decided to nonchalantly declare we weren't getting paid.

'I'm not happy about it, just as I'm not happy that someone has stolen cash from the office.'

Now this was news to me, but I immediately looked at the boys we had travelled with. Two of them were broadcasting the most blatant guilty signals, yet I noticed that Noel was eyeballing me again. Couldn't blame him I guess, but he was wrong. Meanwhile, the fact that the promoter had accused us had sent Liam over the edge. On top of this there was the same large firm from outside gathering to watch proceedings. Now before you could say boo to a goose it's gone right off.

I saw Liam having fisticuffs with some big kid, but Liam was getting the better of him, and Tony was flailing around and actually looked like he was enjoying himself, until I ran over, grabbed the pair of them and headed for the van. We fled through corridors, stumbled into the back of the vehicle and were quickly squashed flat by the rest of the entourage diving in. With a rev and a squeal, we were off. On the way out they were banging the side of the van with sticks and metal bars and bricks were bouncing off the roof. I'm not sure what fucking lubricant the crowd had indulged in that night, but it was one evening I'd never forget.

We drove home, laughing as we recalled the night's events. Everybody was on a high; it had been a good musical performance as well as an eventful evening. I was sat up front in the Transit with Noel as Bonehead drove.

'It had fuck all to do with me, that money Noel. I promise.'

An empty money tin had been found in the van after we had set off.

'You sure?' asked Noel.

'I promise you mate. I don't want to fuck this thing up, I'm having the best days of my life.'

'What do you mean by "this thing"?' he said.

'I mean us, Oasis. I swear Noel, this band is going to be the biggest band to ever come out of Manchester.'

'You're not fucking wrong there, but you need to find yourself something to do, become a drum or guitar technician so you can roadie for us.'

It was good advice, given with good intentions, and I should have listened, but lugging a guitar or heaven forbid Tony's full drum kit around wasn't for me. I was more creative.

'I want to manage the band,' I spluttered out. Noel's response was one of outright laughter, which didn't bode well for the words that were to follow.

'Fuck off Bigun, you'd have us all either in the clink, the ground or a Betty Ford Clinic.'

The rest of the group roared laughing as I considered his words. You know, he was probably right. We drank and smoked our way home without a consideration for the fact we were playing in Oldham the following evening.

That next evening was another progressive performance, as were the six or seven gigs that filled the rest of the year. If we weren't performing, we'd be sat in the basement rehearsal room causing mayhem and carnage throughout the Boardwalk. Life was wild.

Meanwhile, back in the real world, work carried on. I was given a job. Eric Cantona asked me to sort out his motor for him. He had just crossed the Pennines in a controversial transfer from Leeds United and had become an immediate success at United. Just a new tyre was required, he told me in his broken English.

'Sure, it ees no problem,' I offered back in a clumsily cliched French accent; but I don't think he saw the funny side.

I had been using a tyre shop in Salford for a year or so. They were not exactly certified but they were only fitting tyres and were incredibly inexpensive. Me, Liam and Tony headed there one lunch time, rolling through Manchester like we owned it. Eric's huge black Mercedes was top of the range and a right eye-turner. On arrival at the tyre shop we hopped out to whistles and gasps.

'Who the fuck does that belong to? And don't say it's yours,' roared the shop owner, Brian. I laughed. I liked Brian, he was a funny man.

'Big Eric at United,' I told him and his face lit up.

'Ooh Ahh, Cantona's car,' he started to sing, and the rest of the workshop joined in. Like I said, he was a funny man. Two of his grease-monkeys set to work and rolled the vehicle onto an hydraulic lift; bit much to change the tyres I thought, as I left to shoot the breeze with Brian. Before I could even light the end of my Benson there was a large bang, followed by a shriek, followed by another bang.

I spun on my heels and hightailed it into the workshop. I could not even begin to comprehend what I saw. I first noticed Liam and Tony, who were howling laughing and pointing. I followed their fingers. I began to feel ill as I saw, rocking to a halt on the floor of the garage, the front passenger door to Cantona's car. It seemed to be no longer connected to the rest of his car, which was sitting skew whiff on the ramp next to two very apologetic looking mechanics. My head started to swim as I thought of the ramifications of what had just happened. I could faintly hear Brian telling me that he had no insurance and I couldn't claim anyway because of the signs and I was thinking how the fuck do I get out of this? I was still stood in complete disbelief. I really could not believe what I was seeing.

'What the fuck just happened?' I roared incredulously.

'It's the Mercedes, Bigun. It fell off the ramps,' the two mechanics responded in a nervous whisper.

'Yes, I fuckin got that as soon as I spotted the door on the floor but thank you anyway!' I screamed in an uncontrollable rage which brought a cease to Tony and Liam's laughter and a clarity to my mind. The General could fix this.

The General was an old school friend called Jimmy Regan who was a good friend from Levenshulme. He had grown up with us and had always been a keen mechanic. Keen enough that he now owned his own garage and was always good for a favour. So we rolled Cantona's car off the ramp, actually secured his door to the roof, and headed off to see The General. There was no need for air conditioning and both Tony and Liam got the breeze full on from the unblocked doorway.

As I rolled up outside The General's garage, he stood shaking his head at me.

'What the fuck have you been up to now?' he laughed, as I hurriedly explained the magnitude of the fuckwittery that had just occurred. I then explained to The General that he must fix it in the next two hours. He then explained to me that I was a halfwit and it could not happen. He was right on the first count but miraculously wrong on the second. So later that afternoon we returned a modified and reconstructed Mercedes Benz to Mr Eric Cantona with a lesson learnt and an enormous new hole in my bank account.

Although I had learnt my lesson this incident was to come back and bite me on my arse. Coupled with the time Liam had decided to clean Paul Ince's wheel arches with wire wool - yes, wire wool - I was skating on thin ice and I knew it. I sat both Tony and Liam down and told them it was time to switch on, and to their credit they duly did.

Onwards with the band, and we started gigging again at the beginning of 1993. Once more it was the Boardwalk, mainly due to the fact we only had to carry the gear up one flight of stairs and down again. Easy shift. Easy night. The band were sounding better than ever and Liam was ruling the roost on every stage he walked.

It was getting more difficult for us to maintain the boss/employee relationship the more confident he became. That was always going to be the case and it was something I welcomed. It showed he was developing. And boy, the whole band was about to develop.

Noel had arranged for us to go and hang out with another band he had met through the Inspiral Carpets. The Real People were a Scouse four piece act who had a hit in the early nineties with the single 'Windowpane'. It was a trippy guitar affair and I loved it, so was quite excited when Noel told us we were spending the weekend with them at their studio in Bootle.

The band was fronted by two likeable brothers, Chris and Tony Griffiths. They are probably two of the most talented musicians I have come across and to describe them as helpful would be an understatement. I spent the weekend partying and to be honest don't remember a single instrument being hit, plucked or strummed. What I do remember is two intensely passionate musicians dishing out fun, anecdotes, pills, advice and Jack Daniels.

Back in work on the Monday morning we were all feeling the worse for wear. I think Tony was getting it the most as he had a missus and a kid at home, so to go missing for the weekend on a bender wasn't what the other half had in mind when supporting his pursuit of musical success.

'We're back there every Tuesday, Wednesday and Thursday evening. Noel told me this morning,' Liam groaned. He was ashen white with sweat pouring out of him. Nobody was looking forward to work on this day.

The arrangement with The Real People went on for the next two or three months. I found it difficult to attend as it wasn't the weekend, which was okay. When I did attend, it was serious partying and no actual music being played, so I hadn't heard what the band had been working on with the 'Realies'. In fact, I hadn't heard the band for at least two months.

Finally, we were back to normal weekend rehearsals at The Boardwalk. I remember Noel smiling at me as we arrived for our first Boardwalk rehearsal in over two months.

'Got some new tunes,' he announced. 'I want to know what you think.'

I plonked my frame in my chair just to the left of Tony's drum kit.

'Well crack on then, let's hear 'em.'

The band then ran through a set that consisted of 'Columbia' (now with lyrics), 'All Around the World', 'Slide Away', 'Cigarettes and Alcohol', 'Don't Go Away' and 'Up in the Sky'.

I was even more fucking gobsmacked than when Cantona's car door hit the floor. I'm not an emotional man, but right there, right then, I could have cried. The feeling was one of pride and respect. I can honestly say that the moment I heard those songs I knew that the band was destined for stardom. And so did they.

'They're all your own songs?' I asked Noel.

'Yes,' he beamed back.

'Fucking Hell.'

It was like a new band had been born. I could see the look of confidence on every band member's smiling face. Liam's strutting was more pronounced, his voice a snarling rasp rather than the angelic tones of beforehand. And it worked. Boy, did it fucking work.

'Play the set again,' I demanded.

'Really?' asked Noel.

'Yes, really.'

I sat back as the dark ominous tones of 'Columbia' filled the room. The set was even better the second time around. That day the band would also play completely restructured versions of 'Rock'n'Roll Star' and 'Bring It On Down'. Within the next few weeks Noel would add 'Live Forever' and 'Supersonic'. I really was in a daze, as was most of the band. We weren't sounding just good, we were sounding real fucking good, and the journey had to begin. The question was where?

Chapter Seven
You've Got to Make it Happen

Me, Liam and Tony were giving Fergie's car a right old going over. We always went the extra mile on the gaffer's car, for you'd be told if you didn't. The spirits were high, as we only had one other vehicle to do and then come lunch we were off! After a bit of wheeling and dealing we'd provisionally booked ourselves an appearance at King Tuts in Glasgow. We'd hired two vans for the occasion and a night on the tiles was the intention of all once the gig was completed.

After a journey up the M6 in a distillery on wheels, when we arrived in Glasgow, I noticed that most were already mindless. Could be a shitty night in store for us I thought, as even the band were looking more unstable than usual. We started to haul the equipment out of the back of the van only to be stopped by a doorman.

'Woah there pal,' came a thick Scottish accent. The doorman then explained that we couldn't appear that evening as there were already three bands on. This did not go down well with anyone.

'Fuck that mate, we've just driven for the last four bastard hours to get here,' I offered in a tone crying out for a bit of sympathy. When that was ignored the rest of the crowd started hurling threats of violence and arson instead. That seemed to do the trick, and before you knew it we were through the door and propping up the bar.

The crowd was good, although the place was not rammed. I genuinely enjoyed the Oasis concerts around this time. It's like you know just how good your band are so you spend more time watching for the crowd reaction rather than the actual performance. I also began to notice the same people popping up at different gigs. It really was beginning to happen.

That evening the boys were on fire. They had been allowed to play a four song set which included 'Rock'n'Roll Star', 'Bring it on Down' and 'Up in the Sky'. The band had also added a cover of The Beatles track 'I am the Walrus' to the set list. The songs were delivered by Liam in a fully zipped tracksuit, looking ominous and trouble ready. There was an air of menace about the whole performance but one that was intoxicating and enjoyable and the crowd reaction was again one of 'awe'. The boys piled off stage and we began recreational habits at the back of the bar.

Shortly after we were joined by Noel, who announced that he had just been offered a record deal by a chap named Alan McGee. I'd never fucking heard of him but it seemed he had started a record company called Creation Records which had given the world the likes of Primal Scream and The Teenage Fanclub. We'd been offered record deals before but for some reason Noel was extremely excited by this offer and the mood was one of exuberance. Could it finally be happening? We spent the rest of the evening creating low key mayhem as we were under strict orders and sang 'Rock'n'Roll Star' all the way back to Manchester.

The following morning we were back on duty at The Cliff. The comedown from the previous evening was, as always, killing us. Trying to remove tar from a wheel arch doesn't exactly give the same satisfaction as fronting a band through an explosive performance, and from the look on Liam's face you could tell.

'What's up with you, misery arse?'

'Just fucked off.'

'You've just been offered a record contract, what've you got to be fucked off about?' I offered, hoping perspective might lighten his mood.

'I know, I know, but what if it doesn't happen?'

'Fuck worrying about shit like that, it's gonna fuckin happen, have faith in Uncle Bigun.'

The smile had re-appeared and the light had returned to the kid's eyes.

'You're right Pauly, and when we do we're gonna smash the whole country. You know we're going to look after you, don't you? Whatever job you want, it's yours.'

'Let's wait until you're on *Top of the Pops* before you start planning my future fella.' I'd always admired Liam for being a good guy and believe me I was thankful for the opportunity that their talent had given me. But I had always been pragmatic. Let's wait and see what happens.

Well, I didn't need to wait long. I'd always arrange the car cleaning business around the band's engagements, be it rehearsals or performances. Tony or Liam would normally just give me prior notice of a date and I would pencil it in. The following morning Tony turned up with a list. He'd had to write the dates down as there were so many. There was a whole host of performance dates, a trip to Amsterdam, recording time and a planned trip to London to sign a record contract.

I looked at Tony and I smiled.

'We've fucking made it, is this serious?'

Tony smiled back with a look of sheer joy on his face.

'Amsterdam. We're going to Amsterdam,' he laughed. The trip to The Dam was all he was interested in; I guess it summed up all the band's attitude at that precise moment in time.

Right there and then it registered. It was over. The last two years at The Cliff with the players and staff of Manchester United with Liam as my partner in crime were over. I guess I also knew that my time with the band sat in The Boardwalk was also over. I wondered if life would ever be the same again. Never could I have guessed.

As predicted, a couple of days later, both Liam and Tony handed in their notices. It was a strange and sad day but also a day of hope and expectations.

'Gonna miss this place you know,' said Liam.

'Pretty sure they'll miss you as well,' I replied. Liam had become a firm favourite amongst the United players, mainly due to his cheek and ability to put a smile on your face.

'Will you miss it when you leave Bigun? You know, when you come and work with us?'

'I guess I will Liam, I guess I will.'

Although I had agreed to work for the band, I had major reservations about leaving United. It had been my dream to work here and we had become trusted and valuable members of the team down at The Cliff. The daily giggles with the players had become part of my life and one which I enjoyed. The thought of maybe managing Oasis or doing promotional stuff for them was too good to turn down, but I also thought it would be fleeting. So I decided that no matter what happened with the band, my contract with United was far more important to me.

From there on in it was a bit of a whirlwind. The boys jumped on that ferry to Amsterdam on that trip they were so looking forward to. Unfortunately they never reached their destination due to tearing it up on the ferry and getting themselves arrested. Liam was in good spirits on his return though, particularly with regards to the press it received. Then before you know it, Noel decided to just knock out a little ditty called 'Supersonic' and we were in a van on our way to London to perform it on a Channel Four show called *The Word*.

I couldn't believe it and neither could the boys. That night Liam's face was plastered on televisions all across the UK. They'd not even released a record yet it was almost as if they'd released a dozen albums.

Due to this, Liam's house was now getting constant attention through either fans or press so he decided to move in with me on Kettering Road in Levenshulme. This was fine and dandy with me, as looking at his diary for the next three months he'd be staying a total of fourteen nights. Oasis were making waves big time out there and I wished them all the luck in the world.

Liam rang the house one evening and told me he was flying home. He was back for a couple of nights so I arranged to meet in this pub called The Woodstock Arms in Didsbury.

The Woodstock is one of those lovely big old pubs that has a big beer garden surrounded by massive old trees that give shelter from the roads that virtually surround it. It was a hot summer night in 1995 and I was out in the pub garden, excited to be seeing Liam and Noel again and getting on it.

A few pints in already and basking in the evening warmth, I was shooting expectant glances over towards the doors that opened out into the pub garden. Manchester loves it when their lads and lasses do well, especially when it comes to music. I thought the boys would walk in to people inside the pub all wanting to congratulate them, have a photo, maybe get something signed. You know, a bit of a hero's welcome.

They did arrive, and they'd thought the same thing, as they'd been getting it more and more as their success grew; so when I looked over towards the rustling trees at the end of the beer garden and saw the conquering heroes emerge from there, I was gobsmacked. They skipped over a wall by the road that ran along the end of the pub's land, fought through branches and leaves and then walked out into about 300 people holding drinks and staring at them with open mouths.

'Alright Bigun,' Liam and Noel said as they swaggered towards me, full of that attitude they have and grinning from ear to ear. I pissed myself at the shocked looks on people's faces watching the two idiots arrive, picking bits of tree off their clothes. Then, as the realisation dawned on everyone as to who it was that had just materialised through the foliage, I pissed myself some more.

It was surreal, and everyone was buzzing from it. They swaggered over and got a load of drinks in, and then the subject of nose candy came up. They wanted to get some in. It was a celebration, so of course they did.

I knew people back then, so I rang them and made arrangements. While we waited for it to turn up, Noel and Liam were filling me in on what had been going on and who they'd met, who they'd pissed off and who they'd been interviewed by. There was a noticeable change in the atmosphere, and people were all gathering around us, without being too in our faces, but listening in and chuckling, and everyone was loving it. The air was warm, the drinks flowed, the gear turned up; and so me and my old mate Liam popped to the toilets to powder our noses. We had a surreal moment where we realised we hadn't seen each other for six weeks and that they'd been back to America, and IT HAD HAPPENED! The band were exploding and they were my mates. Life was good.

It was about to get better. We walked out of the toilets and were about to go up the steps out to the rest of the crew, when we came face to face with two stunning women. They'd followed us down and wanted to meet Liam. Well, they were all over him, telling him how much they loved Oasis and all that; he was smiling like a Cheshire cat and bathing in the glory. Fair play to him.

'Do you wanna come to a party with us?' they flirted.

'I'm fucked man, I can't; I've only just got back from America. I've got jetlag,' Liam responded, sounding all rock starry.

I gave Liam a dig in the ribs and a meaningful look that asked what the hell he was doing.

'Yeah, OK,' he told them, 'we can come for an hour or so.' Their eyes lit up and they did that squealing and clapping hands thing excited women do, while jumping up and down in heels. Liam and I looked at each other and raised an eyebrow, wordlessly sharing the same thoughts based entirely on filthy minds.

We didn't tell Noel or anyone else and just followed them out, listening only to the devil on our shoulders who was whispering terrible yet enjoyable suggestions. The women excitedly led us out to their car, which surprisingly was an old Triumph Spitfire. Not the biggest car in the world by any standards. Liam jumped in the back with one of them and I squeezed in the front with the other one, who was driving.

It was about 11pm at night, it was the height of summer and we had the roof down and were loving life. So off we zoomed with our two new glamorous female friends down to Sale in Trafford. We finally arrived there and parked on a big drive in front of a massive house. As we approached the front door, we could hear Bob Marley playing loudly inside, clearly audible through the multitude of open windows. Liam and I exchanged questioning glances, but we just shrugged and went with it.

In we walked. And we'd never seen anything like it. As we surveyed the smoky scene in front of us, we realised that there must have been 200 Rastafarians in the place. It was a bloody big house, but 200 people were filling it up and I think every one of them must've had a massive spliff in their mouths. The air was thick with pungent smoke. Liam seemed a bit on edge by this point, and I didn't really know what to make of it. Manchester's a pretty good multicultural city, and we were good with all races. That said, it was a bit daunting by anyone's standards.

Everyone had clocked us coming in and had been staring. Liam was looking shifty as hell, and I tried to remain stony faced, but inwardly wondering if we'd made a mistake here. The feeling increased when quite a few of the partygoers started coming towards us, squinting at us closely through the smoky haze. Just as we were about to turn tail and leg it, one guy came up to Liam, clapped him on the shoulder, smiled and said in patois: 'Cooh deh! Yeah, Liam maaan. Dah bredda is de Gallagher brother, man.'

The place erupted in joyous shouts of happy things neither me nor Liam understood; but what a vibe! At that point everyone was on Liam, laughing and talking to him, welcoming him to their party. It was great to watch. Liam didn't know how to react at first, but got into it and loved this surreal welcome from the most unexpected of audiences. You know you've made it when early doors in your career you've got half of the Bob Marley fan base on your side. Like I said, Manchester celebrates their kin doing well. Whatever their colour or creed, people in Manchester were rooting for Oasis.

Well, we stayed at the party most of the night with our newfound friends. We listened to reggae, laughed, smoked weed and had a blast. When we finally toddled off in the daylight hours the next day, we kept looking at each other and grinning at the weirdest night we'd just had. The girls lived in Sale and left us to grab a taxi, so we didn't get our kicks there. Not a bother; we'd had a cracking night and it showed how much of a legend Liam was becoming.

Chapter Eight
A Hurricane Comes to Town

So, everywhere I went everybody wanted to know about Oasis. It was mind blowing, and I thought things could not get any more hectic. I was wrong.

There was a period of my life when I had an aptly nicknamed man stay with me who temporarily threw my life into further turmoil than it was already in.

He was a man known as Alex 'Hurricane' Higgins. He was deserving of the name, as that's exactly what he was like as far as I was concerned: a hurricane. A human whirlwind. A force of nature. He turned up, turned everything upside down, turned around, and then left.

That wasn't why he was called nicknamed Hurricane, though. He earned that moniker because of how fast he would play snooker, the craft he had honed. He was the snooker World Champion in 1972 and 1982, and runner-up in 1976 and 1980. He was also one of only nine players to have completed snooker's Triple Crown. He was also a lovely man and another right pain in the arse. I certainly seemed to attract a certain type.

Mike Lester, another West Point stalwart, had been driving him to snooker matches and appointments. This was at the stage when it was fairly evident to all concerned that he was giving up on soldiering on, if you get my meaning. He was struggling in life and had been battling his demons. He'd recently been through a messy divorce and was leaning on friends and acquaintances as well as substances and booze. In short, he was starting to give up, and he was looking very much worse for wear.

Alex had been holed up at the place of this mutual friend that was driving him, but he had to go off for reasons that I can no longer remember, and he asked if I could put him up for a couple of weeks. I wasn't entirely keen on the idea, but I agreed, nonetheless. What could go wrong? I laugh at thinking that now.

Liam had moved out of my place, as he finally had some money coming in and had managed to sort his own place out, so I found myself with an often empty flat and a spare bedroom. So, Alex moved in and took Liam Gallagher's old bedroom. You couldn't make this up: world famous snooker player takes the bedroom of the world famous rock star in a little flat I'd shared with half of Oasis!

At the time, Alex was in a pretty bad place mentally, but I thought a bit of stability might do him good. Plus, I thought it'd be a buzz and an injection of life, especially as I was now seeing less and less of Liam and the Oasis boys, although Liam and Tony still popped back when the meteoric success they were experiencing allowed them.

So, one day, the famous and infamous Hurricane Higgins turned up on my doorstep with a sports bag full of his gear and a whole load of Irish chat. Admittedly, we did have a lot of fun together, but he was also one of the most unpredictable people I've met in my fairly tempestuous life. When anyone did come around while he was under the same roof as me, they normally encountered some farce or another; a comedy of errors starring Bigun and Alex Higgins!

One night when he was round mine, and I was in the middle of a particularly crappy bout of flu (not man flu, the real deal I'll have you know), he told me that he had a great old cure for it and that he could get me feeling right as rain in no time at all. Thinking he was going to sort me out with an ancient Irish cure, steeped in magic from the Emerald Isle and honed to perfection over hundreds of years, I readily agreed.

He got me to sit at the dining table and then carefully walked in with a massive steaming bowl of boiling hot water. As he approached me, I assumed the pungent steam coming from it must be a herbal remedy passed from generation to generation through his family, shrouded in secret, and that he must be about to impart it to me.

You know what it was? Olbas Oil. It was a bowl of boiling water and Olbas Oil. Of course, I found this out later, but at the time I was sure it was something exotic and powerful.

At the time though, it all seemed very nice and quite touching, to be honest; and I told Alex so. He just smiled, ceremoniously placed the bowl in front of me and then handed me a towel. He then proceeded to explain that I needed to breathe in the vapours with the towel over my head acting as a shroud to keep in the fragrant and healing steam.

So he helped me place the towel over my head, then I leaned over the bowl on the table in front of me and deeply breathed in the herbal steam. There I was, feeling comforted and surprised at this touching gesture from Alex, when he suddenly put a hand at the back of my head and pushed my face into the extremely-near-boiling water! The pain was immediate, and immense, and so was my reaction. I exploded, calling him all the names under the sun and pulling the towel off my head whilst looking round to see where the mischievous bastard had gone to.

I heard our front door slam. He'd bloody run out of the house! As soon as he dunked my face in the steaming water, he knew I'd go ballistic, so he ran away. I ran down the street after him, while he was cackling like the lunatic I often thought he really was and I was calling him every swear word I could muster. As I ran after him, I could feel my nose swelling up where it had dipped into the scalding water. I had a blister on it for days afterwards and looked a right idiot, I can tell you.

I didn't catch him then, but after an hour or so, I began to laugh about it. It had been a dangerous thing to do, but yes, it was funny. More importantly, I decided that I had to exact my revenge upon the cheeky little Irish bastard. But here's the thing. That man was so clued up, so sharp in his thinking, that I never really got him back for what he did. Not properly on that level where someone ends up with an injury. He was always on his guard. That said, I did royally stitch him up once without him knowing about it.

What he never knew never hurt him. And one of those things he was oblivious to was when he was at the flat and he got up one morning with a craving for some weed. Not just any weed, it was a strain called 'bush'. He was depressed and thought it might help him get out of his funk. Personally, I wouldn't touch that shit and think it's the last thing you need when on a downer as it's a downer itself, but I also knew what he was like when he wanted something. He was like a spoilt child at those times.

The thing is, it transpired that no one had any bush. This wasn't Amsterdam where I could choose from a dizzying selection off a menu in a smoke-filled coffee shop. This was Moss Side and that wasn't something readily available. So I told him I couldn't get it, and was surprised at the explosive reaction when he came back telling me that I could fucking get it if I really tried and that he needed it right there and then. He was shouting and properly angry. I didn't take kindly to be spoken to like that in my own home, so I concocted a plan to get the petulant Irish bastard.

There was a girl I knew in a flat opposite called Joanne, so I went and asked if she could be part of my cunning plan to sort Alex out, and get me some much needed and overdue revenge. It wasn't on the level of dunking someone's face in boiling water, but it would appease the Gods of Payback to an extent. I asked her to go to the supermarket and get one of those big bargain bags of mixed herbs and some other shit to mix with it, then put it in a sealable bag so that it looked like something fittingly dodgy. So she did all this for me and came back to secretly drop it off at mine.

I put on a decent show of proudly presenting Alex with it, and said that I'd managed to sort him out, good and proper, like, as only a real mate would. I'd been over to Moss Side, I told him, and there I had I met up with a right dodgy bastard with a big van and had finally sourced some of his much needed bush. Naturally this had all been done with the ever-present threat of danger to myself and possibly death. Man, I laid it on thick. He was all the more appreciative for it.

Well, you should have seen his little face light up. I left him to his devices with his bag of weed, and in a few minutes came back to see him filling a seven skinner up with what he believed to be his desired heady and potent mix. I just about managed to hold the laughter back as he proceeded to light up his huge faux-spliff and puff away on it with a contented and sated look upon his face. A proper placebo effect.

Although the house stank for days afterwards, it was worth it as he actually chilled the hell out for a while, waxing lyrically about what good shit it was. Just goes to show how psychologically effective a placebo can be. And stinky. Bloody hell that stuff reeked to high heaven!

Although he was effectively living in Liam's old bedroom, he hadn't met Liam until one night when he came back to the flat, and there sat me, Liam, Coatsy and Heath. As Alex walked in, Liam was sat in the chair next to me, and Alex walked over to the other side of the room with his hand held out and introduced himself to Heath, thinking he was Liam. Heathy laughed and pointed over to where Liam was actually sat. How he had missed the news stories and pictures, I do not know; but he certainly didn't know what he looked like.

'I'm over 'ere, ya daft bastard,' Liam laughed after seeing him make this faux pas, and so they finally met in a flurry of masculine Mancunian posturing and Irish bravado.

That night, we all bundled into two cars after someone suggested we go down to a club in Stockport for a few beers together. At the time it was a place called Grand Central, but people will know it now as Heaven and Hell. At the time, Liam and Oasis must have been on their third single and he was becoming properly famous and was getting recognised; especially in Manchester. Meanwhile, Alex Higgins was already famous around the world and was obviously perceived as a bit of a legend.

We arrived, already on our way to being hammered. The rest of us walked a few paces behind Liam and Alex. We all watched them as they strutted into this place, which was pretty full up. You can imagine what it was like. There were the music lovers and there were the sports lovers. Then there were the people who loved both, who were like dogs with two tails! Our lads were both lapping up the attention, of course. Liam went full swagger and Alex started to unleash his Irish ol' blarney charm offensive, getting drinks bought for him. They were absolutely loving it, both of them.

Then, before you know it, they both had queues of people lining up to get autographs from them, in a very typically British well-mannered way. So, bolstered by the attention, Liam and Alex started comparing the lengths of their queues saying that each had more fans than the other, counting how many there were in line to just have a word, or get something signed. This was before the days of camera phones, otherwise it would have been selfies everywhere. In those days it was the shake of a hand, a kiss, and possibly get a signature if you had something to write on.

Let it be noted for the record: at that time, it was Liam that had the longest queue. Understandably with the whole Manchester thing that on that night, as the returning hero, he happened to have the biggest dick in a dick competition. That said, old Hurricane Higgins held his own, and I'm sure he had Liam worried there. It only went to show that there was so much love for the man wherever he went; but unfortunately, that didn't help him battle his depression.

The darker side to Alex was displayed one night when he'd said that he was off out down Stockport Road in Levenshulme, a road that had a number of pubs and clubs. I wasn't his keeper in the few months he was with me, so I said 'see ya later' as he left the flat and didn't think anything of it.

Like I said, he'd hit hard times. Little did I know that he was off out with the intentions of going down a working men's club playing pool for people to place bets on. Unfortunately, those bets were naturally going to be on the legend and former world champion, Hurricane Higgins, beating the best players in the club. Who in their right mind would bet on him losing?

Unbeknownst to them, Alex was having a quiet word with his opponents and effectively throwing the games for a cut of the money having placed his own reversed bet. This evidently went well for a while, until someone picked up on him cheating. Now, in his defence, when you're desperate, you can find yourself doing desperate things without a thought for the inevitable outcome.

So, he got found out, and the people were after his blood. The ones who had been duped, that is. You can kinda see their point, really. Who would YOU bet on? A geezer from the working men's club, or a World Champion snooker player?

Now, this hadn't happened in a nice little middle-class eatery or wine bar. This was a working men's club in Levenshulme. The clientele weren't the most savoury of characters, nor were they the most forgiving.

They were all after him. He did a runner outside and jumped into a nearby bush. Of course, he got on his mobile phone and who did he call to come sort it out? The Bigun, that's who! I was asleep but picked up the call that had woken me up. It was half past midnight by this time, and he said that there was a guy there who wanted to kill him and asked if I could be his knight in shining armour. Of course, I had to go save him, despite me being pretty much at the end of my tether with him. Annoyed with him or not, I couldn't let him get a beating. There wasn't much left of him these days, so I'm pretty sure he wouldn't have done too well in a fight.

I asked him where he was. He said he was at the Klondike Club, hiding in a bush outside, reiterating that people wanted him dead. I'd got that.

It's a good job I hadn't been out on the sauce, as I hammered down there in my motor, screeched to a halt outside in a cloud of scorched rubber and found myself instantly grappling with a geezer that was feeling a tad put out from the cunning ruse the Irish legend had inflicted upon him! He was like a bear with a sore head, who behind him was backed up by several smaller bears with equally sore heads.

Realising now that the situation could actually turn quite serious for the two of us, I chose my moment and ended up bundling Alex into the car, then wheel spinning away in a cloud of tyre smoke and volley of angry bricks that our antagonists had somehow got hold of. The lovable idiot didn't go back there, needless to say.

There's one thing for sure though. The boy lived his life, no one could deny that. Things turned worse for him, of course. I was with him the day he was diagnosed with cancer. I took him to the private clinic that had been kindly paid for by Jimmy White. Jimmy, nicknamed 'The Whirlwind', was a finalist in World Championship Snooker, famous for losing in the final six times in a row. He was also a former World Doubles champion with Alex Higgins and a great friend of his. It must have been killing him to see his mate fall on hard times and then bad health.

So, we both went to this posh BUPA place that was more like a hotel than a medical centre. At his request, I stayed in the car when he went in to get the test results, and I knew what the answer was when I saw him come out and climb back into the car. He didn't need to say it, but he did say it.

He sighed, and like a broken man, said, 'I've got throat cancer.' It was the beginning of his end.

He left Manchester not long after that and carried on like he wasn't ill; he partied hard like he was a youngster. Unfortunately, he died back in Belfast twelve years later, a shadow of his former self, but his legend lives on.

Alex 'Hurricane' Higgins brought snooker to a different audience, a younger audience. He made it cool to like snooker and he will always be remembered for that. He was top man, a proper pain in the arse, and I was proud to call him my friend. He was, and still is, sorely missed.

Chapter Nine
Fergie Puts the Boot in

I was with Liam in Manchester. We'd had to change the way we operated due to the fact that he was probably now one of the most recognisable faces in the country. So it was dark corners of quiet boozers or walks in the hills surrounding Manchester for a smoke and a conversation. Today we had chosen Arnfield reservoir, in Tintwistle, to walk around.

'How's everyone at United?' he asked. Although an avid Blue he had made a lot of friendships during those times.

'Everyone's good, they're always asking about you.'

'I was talking about being there in an interview Bigun, I told them about you and Cantona's car. Oh, and Paul Ince's.' He laughed.

'Brill, that's going to go down well with Fergie,' I replied sarcastically.

Liam laughed it off. 'Don't worry, you're gonna get looked after by us. Just give it a couple of months.'

I was more concerned about the reaction at United than getting looked after by the boys. I considered it an honour and an accolade to work at Manchester United and made a serious point of trying not to cock it up, despite some hooligans working for me trying to do the exact opposite.

So, the following Friday, I was minding my own business, literally, up at the training ground known as The Cliff in sunny

Salford. As I pulled up to the large red gates, security told me, in very ominous tones, 'The Gaffer wants to see you.'

This was not welcome news. The Gaffer at the time was Alex Ferguson, or Fergie as he's affectionately known. You know, with him being such a warm-hearted individual that you can't help but love... ha! Believe me, that is not the case.

Alex Ferguson (Sir Alex to you) is the longest ever serving manager at Manchester United Football Club, having overtaken Sir Matt Busby's tenure in 2010. Fergie eventually retired after 26 years' service at the club and is not known for pulling his punches or for ever being too far away from controversy.

Such as with the infamous incident in a dressing room argument with David Beckham when he kicked a football boot in anger which then hit Becks right in his face. As I say, his short fuse was no secret and everyone at Man United trod carefully around him. Everyone. Including me.

So, I knew he had a volcano-like temper. And I'd just been told that he wanted to see me. Brilliant.

My heart sank. You know that feeling when you're a kid? That anxiety and fear when someone you hold in high regard due to their authority, or someone you are just plain scared of, hauls you in? Well, it was like that. But ten times worse. My livelihood was attached to it.

I parked up, and with heavy heart I started to make my way to his office. Like a dead man walking I trudged through reception and towards what I considered my inevitable doom, when I suddenly bumped into Lee Sharpe. This didn't help.

Sharpe laughed out loud: 'He's gonna have you, mate! He's in a right stinker.'

I asked: 'What for though? What's happened?'

He continued his laughter. 'Something to do with match tickets.'

Now this lifted me, as I thought he obviously hadn't read about the Cantona incident, and I figured that maybe, just maybe, I could blag my way out of it. I decided if it was just handing out tickets then that wasn't too serious; I'd charm my way out of that. Surely?

A little bolstered by this, I ran up the stairs and knocked on his door.

'Come in!' came a fierce Glaswegian accent as the door was yanked wide. It didn't sound happy. Then again, Fergie never sounded happy.

A rather flustered and busy looking Fergie stood in front of me as the phone on his desk rang.

He briskly said, 'I'll be a minute,' and shut the door again before I had a chance to step inside his office; leaving me stood like a naughty schoolboy outside the headmaster's office. It felt familiar, I can tell you.

I was stood there, shitting myself, whilst the rest of the United squad passed by. The players all knew me and so the banter was flowing. They couldn't miss this opportunity and walked past throwing out piss-taking quips.

Roy Keane said to me, 'You're a fucking bad boy, you are,' as he walked past.

Jesus, I thought, even Roy Keane is calling me a bad boy. It's funny now, but at the time, I didn't need it!

'Shut it, bomb chucker,' I murmured back, but Roy heard and glared at me over his shoulder. I gave him a nervous smile back. Can't take a joke that fella.

Then Mark Hughes arrived, Sharpe again, and one by one all of the squad traipsed by, tipping me off that Ferguson was gonna have me on this, have me on that and then on the other.

It was Giggsy's turn. His banter was bearable but the content not as much. It confirmed that Ferguson knew all about the Cantona episode.

By now, my heart was in my mouth, as I knew what was coming. I knew exactly what was coming. I was out of the club and I knew it. I felt sick.

Whoosh! The door was ripped open again and I heard those dreaded, coarse Scottish tones: 'Get in here now!'

So I walked in, shaking and in a cold sweat. The first thing I thought was, 'How the hell has he got back in his chair already after just opening that door?'

Fergie had somehow managed to get sat behind his desk on the other side of the room. I figured he must have a remote control or something. Or maybe a teleportation machine. It's strange what goes through your head when you're shitting yourself.

Anyway, I stood there and I was ready to say what I'd got to say. A charm offensive; if that was what it would take, that was what he'd get. *C'mon Bigun, you can do this, you're ready!* Ready as I'd ever be, anyway.

Fergie turned around in his chair and took a deep breath, then said: 'Reet...'

And then his fucking phone rang again! It was killing me. It was torture. He answered, and started angrily bollocking someone else in front of me. I didn't know who it was, other than it being a young player. He told him that he'd fucked this or that up, and I was standing there clenching and unclenching, sweating and shaking, waiting and watching as the man ripped some poor innocent a new hole. And I was next. He hung up the phone.

I was numb, mouth dry, lips stuck to my teeth. He turned around and looked at me, and spotted that I was looking at the crest on the wall. The Manchester United crest. In truth, I was just looking at anywhere that wasn't at him.

He pointed at the crest and said: 'This is Manchester United, son.'

I said, 'Oh, right,' like I didn't know. I didn't really know what else he wanted from me.

Fergie studied me then continued: 'I hev nae nonsense in this club, son. Nae fecking nonsense. Yet I hear yer've bin at it with ma boys.'

'What do you mean?' I asked, genuinely confused.

'Yer've fecking bin oot in the nightclubs, with Sharpey and Giggsy. I know.'

'No, I haven't,' I said, genuine, like.

'You fecking hiv, so don't fecking lie tae me, I've got spies everywhere,' he hissed back.

He was starting to get a little redder in the face now and I was concerned where the spittle on his lips might fire if he started roaring at me.

In my gentlest tones I said, 'Mr Ferguson,' - or maybe Sir Alex, Fergie, who knows - 'this is simply not true. If I go to the Hac and I see Ryan or Lee with their mates or whatever, I'll go up and shake their hands, ask them if they are having a good'un, make idle chat, you know. But that's it. I'll then get my drink and keep away from them.' I told him that because that's exactly how it was.

'Nae you fecking don't. And yer've bin in there with those fecking Gallagher brothers.'

Well, he obviously wasn't having any of it. I was definitely in trouble.

And then more anger spilled out. 'And what the feck is this? What did they scratch on Cantona's car?'

As I dodged the spittle he reached onto his desk and pulled out his smoking gun in the shape of a newspaper. He held it aloft and glared at me. I felt like I was being aggressively interviewed by a stressed-out Taggart.

I spluttered, 'Look, all I can tell you is that this kid Liam worked for me as a valeter,' as I was trying to blag it now. I said, 'Now he's gone off, but I'm still here. I can't help what he's saying, and anyway, that is just newspaper bullshit. He did not scratch Eric Cantona's car and that is a fact.'

The last sentence hit home, and I could see Fergie relax a touch as he pondered. In more measured tones he finally asked, 'So, yer saying that the boy niver even scritched the car?'

I was at that moment. That moment where I knew my next statement would be the lighting taper to the firework. No choice I guess, so sheepishly I offered, 'No, I'm saying he never scratched Cantona's car.' I paused as Fergie lifted his eyebrows reconsidering the options and then I threw in, 'It was Paul Ince's car that he scratched.'

Boom, it was the fuckin Fifth of November as Fergie exploded. 'See I'm not fecking having any of this. Yer fecking off. You're not to come here again. Go on, get oot of ma sight.'

And there were those words. The words I had dreaded. My heart sank, my belly flipped inside. I felt devastated. I was absolutely gutted, man. I was out.

After an emotional farewell to the staff and players I found myself reflecting on the day's events alone, by the side of the River Mersey. United was my club. I'd been there seven years working my proverbials off, building my little empire; building my reputation. Above all, I was building my links with my team. My

Manchester United. This was huge to me. And this place and time was, for me, one of the most integral and defining moments in the change of attitude and ambition of a young Liam Gallagher. It was where he'd be at his happiest and most content. I knew that Liam felt comfortable in the presence of success and had decided he wanted a part of it for himself. I felt proud to have nurtured that and the fact it was part and parcel of Oasis and me, a catalyst for things to happen. Great things.

This is where it came to be, that whole magic of '92. When all of the United starlets were beginning their rise to sporting glory as Champions of England and Europe. And me and Liam Gallagher were there to witness it. So, for me, that's when it was all born. When Liam Gallagher was born. There was a definitive sea change within him. The confidence it gave him, the young kid that didn't have his dad or a brother to relate to. That time and place gave him all these new and interesting people. Successful people. It was all part and parcel of what made him.

Needless to say, I never returned to Manchester United, which saddens me to this day. I did, however, meet Sir Alex Ferguson about six months later when he visited Platt Lane, Manchester City's training ground.

He walked up to me like nothing had ever happened and said, 'Hello. You alright, Paul? Behaving yourself?'

I thought, what kind of acid is this fella on? Is he for fucking real, this guy? I was proper angry at the time and I felt like giving him a clip. I'd cleaned his car for four years, for free I hasten to add. And never a thank you. Although each time I did give him the freebie, I'd always copied the betting coupons he left in his car. Even then the horses never won so I guess I had better resign myself to getting turned over by Fergie no matter which way I go at it!

I am still heartbroken to this day about this episode in my life, but I understand why, as the manager, he had to be seen to be doing what he did. It was his job to protect the players and ultimately protect his beloved football club.

And I'm glad I didn't punch him that day. Reckon there's a good chance he would have beat me like I was a newborn baby. Fierce.

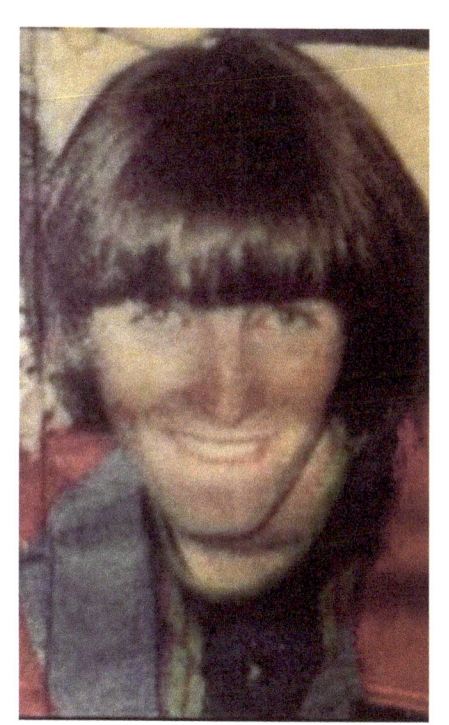

Rock star in the making. Liam Gallagher 15 years old

Tony McCarroll and the drum kit in my pad in Kettering Rd, Levenshulme

Liam and his first love, Cerise

Oasis on stage. Heineken festival 1994

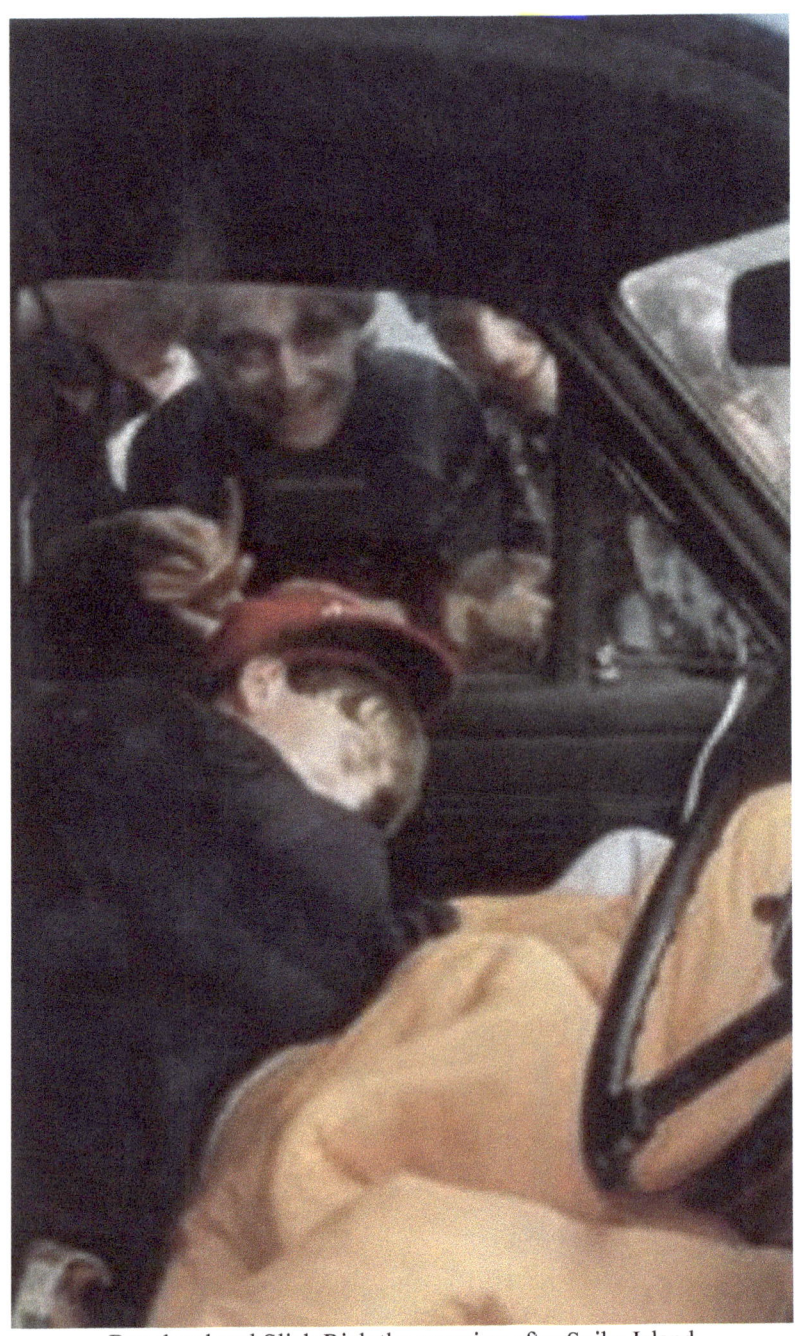

Bonehead and Slick Rick the morning after Spike Island

Me, Spike Island hovering above bottom left: Paul McGuigan (original bass playere in Oasis) and former Rain singer Chris Hutton

Me and Liam in 2011 in the Lowry Hotel. First time I'd seen him in 5 years

Me out joy riding in David Beckhams Ferrari

Liam and me at the Hilton Hotel, Manchester, on the night Man City were celebrating their first premiership

Me, Ricky Hatton and Geo Kinkladze

Me and Gary Neville

Me and Wes Brown at Radcliffe Borough FC training ground

Me and Paul Scholes at a charity footy match

Me and Ricky Hatton st his recent 40th birthday bash at the Ethihad

Me and Bez back stage at the black grape 2014

Lance Clark an me in the street 2014

Me, John Scott and John Morrin living the dream in London, 1986

Me and Mani, Stone Roses, very drunk in Toms Bar, Heaton Moor

Me and Liam shacking it up in 2011

George Kinkladze with my daughter, Emily, who is now 17

My youngest daughter, Lily Jean, giving it the Bigun in Steven Irelands famous Bentley

Emily and Lauren together

Me and Gem Archer, Oasis

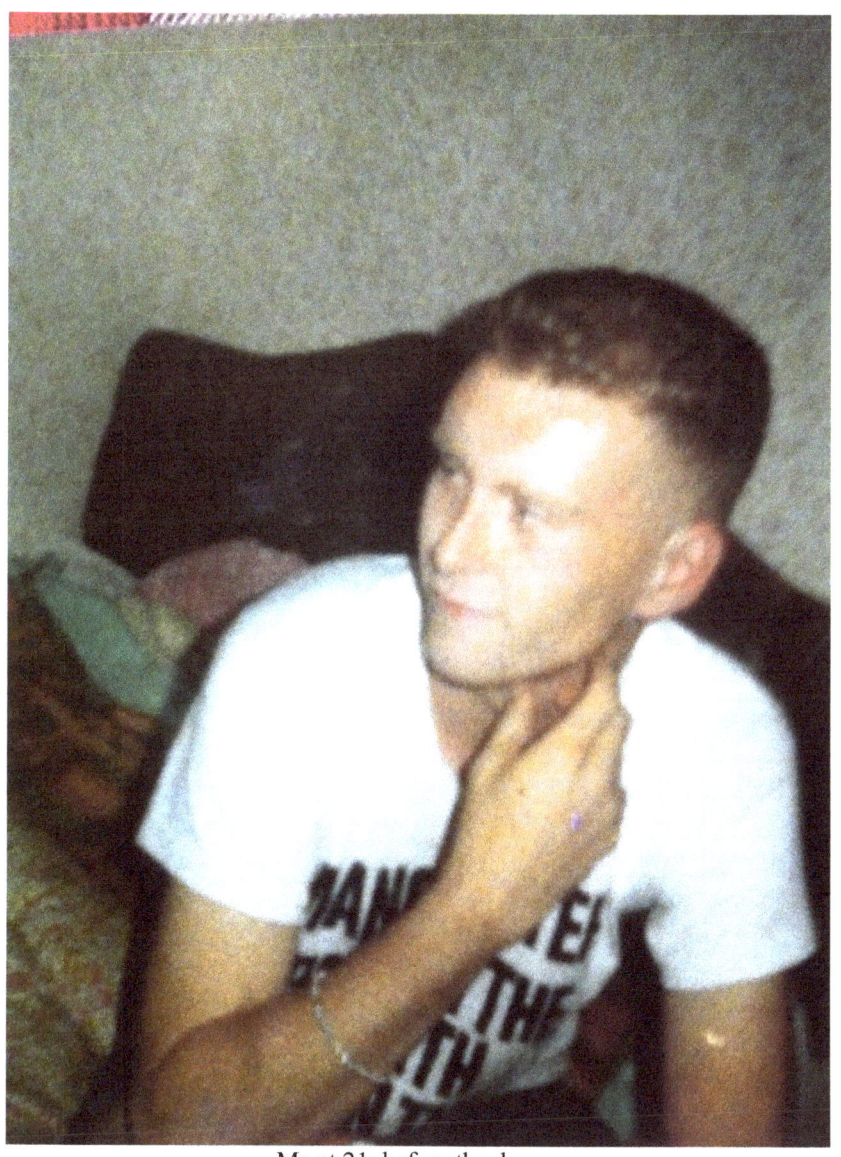

Me at 21, before the dream

Me and Andrew Flintoff at a recent charity football match

The first real time meeting Alan McGee at the black grape concert in 2014

A trip to Beckhams to valet his cars with a young Kane Mallileu

Kinkladze 1995

Chapter 10
Georgian England

I was not happy with Liam. He knew it and circled for a few days. Finally there was a knock on my front door.

'Hiya mate.' He stood, arms outstretched, looking for a bear hug.

I simply turned and walked back inside leaving the front door open.

'Look, I'm sorry, I didn't know you would get the heave-ho over it.'

Liam had cut straight to the chase. He had obviously been informed about what had happened. To be honest though, my firing had been somewhat softened by a new opportunity at Manchester City. I told Liam not to worry about the newspaper article, and about the City job, and he was genuinely excited.

'If this goes tits up can I come back and work for you?' he asked. He was actually being genuine.

'Liam, this is it for you. This is your life. You were born to entertain, not clean cars.'

As modest as ever, Liam laughed. 'Fair point.' And we were back on track. We decided to meet up with Tony Mc and head into town for a session. It was always good when the old firm was reunited.

I was sat at home one evening when Liam turned up at the door. He was not happy. I'd noticed that things were beginning to change around the band. Noel had definitely taken charge and Liam was not reacting well. I'd always remembered his reaction when he watched Noel having his shirts rolled in to a hotel on a rolling wardrobe shortly after the deal had been signed. We were booked into a Travelodge further down the road and were stood in the gruds we'd be going home in.

'What the fuck is going on?' he had reacted angrily.

I had laughed. Noel had always had that edge about him, never really a care for what others thought.

I told Liam that I had been getting mithered off the press both at home and at work but he laughed it off, quite rightly. My attention was minuscule compared to the hounding he was under.

I calmed Liam down by saying that things were bound to change; it was the consequence of being successful. Although that may well have been the case, even then the cracks in the relationship between Noel and Liam were appearing.

Due to my unforeseen non-employment situation I was off on tour with the boys, but with nothing agreed as to my actual role in the band. This meant it would be difficult to pay me anything.

'I'll speak to Noel,' Liam said grudgingly.

I knew Liam didn't have the authority to authorise anything and so did he. In the meantime, I'd just have to plod on. Noel had already advised me on the only options open to me and neither were appealing.

Over the next few days the press intrusion got even more intense. Finally, I spoke to a reporter. He offered me five hundred quid upfront to speak about Liam. Would see me through the tour I thought, so I rattled on about Liam and Noel for a few minutes. Nothing explosive and all positive. Or so I thought.

Liam went ballistic as soon as I told him.

'You've done fucking what?' he raged.

'Gone to the press, just like you fucking did,' I retaliated.

I was not happy, as I felt that what was good for the goose was good for the gander. So I fired back at Liam and he fired back at me until we both calmed down. I left on friendly terms but with an uneasy feeling hanging over me.

Anyway; to more pressing matters. I started my new job as official car valeter for Manchester City FC. It was quite a turnaround and took some getting used to. The first few weeks were quiet, not the same not having Liam and Tony around.

A few months later though a quiet and withdrawn young Georgian arrived in Manchester to play for Manchester City Football Club. He went by the name of Georgi Kinkladze and brought his own unique, graceful and exhilarating style of play to a set of supporters who had never witnessed such before. An instant legend was born. And a new friend made.

His arrival at the training ground on a wet Tuesday morning was greeted by grunts and quick handshakes from his new team mates. The side at that time had very little knowledge of Kinkladze or his footballing talents. Georgi had been signed on the back of one repeatedly watched VHS videotape that had been handed to the Chairman at that time, Francis Lee. It didn't take the team long though, after the start of their training match, to realise that something completely different and very special had arrived.

I watched as the little fella, who couldn't speak a word of English, simply danced around the pitch as if he owned it. The ball, which would often bobble about on the uneven and hard Platt Lane pitch, instead seemed to be superglued to the tip of his boot. The speed in which he left the City defence behind must have been in one way very encouraging for the manager, although from a defensive point of view quite alarming.

After the training session I sauntered over to the smiling and panting Gio and being the chatty chap that I am, I got to talking with him. Naturally, with him being new to the area, I felt it necessary offer my services and explain what vibrant company I am should he happen to fancy a bit of dinner. This message was delivered to him by a very sceptical looking interpreter.

So, after his agreement, and him giving me the name of the hotel he was temporarily staying at, I bowled up later that evening to pick him up. After Gio (through his ever-present translator) made me aware that he had a love for Italian food, I decided that Demetrio's on Dickenson Road in Longsight would be as good a place as any. I knew the food there was good. A pasta carbonara and a slice of tiramisu later Gio was declaring his love for the place.

It became his second kitchen and it wasn't long before we were a regular dining couple.

More often than not though playing gooseberry would be Nicky Summerbee, who had become a father figure for Gio, and he would roar laughing as Gio finally came out of his shell and revealed a serious obsession with playing pranks. Unfortunately for me it seemed that I was to be his main target for such japes, although to be honest if it kept the little fella happy and content it was not a problem.

So, I take my seat in Demetrio's and order a plate of salad. Now the closest I usually get to a salad is when I'm knocking it off the top of a doner kebab but I'm on a get fit regime and need to shift some pounds. I crunch into a leaf of lettuce and then force shredded carrot into me. My usual complaint about salad is that it is just too bland, but not today. Today my salad seems to contain the fieriest taste I've ever experienced and as Gio erupts into squeals of laughter I make a bug-eyed rush for the gentlemen's toilets.

And so it began. I was soon to find that the shy and unassuming young Georgian had an infectiously wicked side as his 'pranks' went to another level. I found superglue where hair gel should have been, and hundreds of taxi drivers and pizza delivery boys at the door. It was as if he had read the stereotypical tabloid reports of players' behaviour and considered them the norm.

One warm Sunday evening I, Gio and Nicky Summerbee arrived at Demetrio's. Gio had played a stormer the previous day and spirits were high. The euphoria though was sucked out of us by a very solemn looking Demetrio who was waiting for us at the door to his restaurant.

'Jeez, Demetrio you alright?' I asked, as the poor fellow seemed hardly able to hold himself upright. I put my arm round him just to be sure.

'It's Mama. She has left us.' With these heavily accented words Demetrio started to wail like a banshee. And wail he did. After the group looking at each other, unsure of what to do, I felt compelled to give him a little shake and the wailing soon reduced to a whimpering.

Demetrio explained that his mother had died the previous morning leaving nothing, not even enough money for her own burial. Now although this started alarm bells ringing loudly - surely a successful restaurant owner such as Demetrio would have looked after his dear old mother? - those bells were not heard by Gio.

I learnt over time that when Gio considered you a friend he'd give you his heart and his soul. There were no half measures involved and he certainly wasn't going to leave Demetrio abandoned in his darkest hour.

Four hours later yours truly was trundling down Kingsway with an envelope containing ten thousand pounds in cash. It seemed that Demetrio had not only himself to fly back to Italy but his very extended family as well. I told Gio again that it wasn't right, but he simply asked me to trust his judgement.

I arrived at the restaurant, where again Demetrio was waiting outside. This time though his face was alight with excitement and anticipation. I hopped out of the car.

'Demetrio, how are we feeling?'

The grieving restaurant owner's face lit up.

'You have the money?'

He was obviously over the worst of it, but I had expected at least some form of pretence. Instead he became visibly excited at the arrival of the envelope as I pulled it out of my jacket. Now it may have been relief that he could go home to Italy and bury his mother, or it may have been he was just an amateur blagger. My money was certainly on the latter as I reluctantly handed over the money.

'When are you back Demetrio?' I knew that Demetrio had arranged a repayment plan with Gio and had promised him a lump sum upon his return.

'I should be back this time next week. Tell Gio that I thank and respect him for this.'

I looked him straight in the eye as he told me this, but he didn't flicker; he was as cool as a breeze. He pocketed the cash and with a crooked and yellow smile he was gone.

The following evening I was at Gio's house in Hale. Gio had begun a relationship with a highly spirited Scouse girl called Joanne and after an evening out we all ended up back at Gio's for an impromptu party. We were lounging in the main room with the Georgian contingent seriously outdoing all other nationalities in the drinking games and general lunacy.

Gio had that mischievous look about him but he also seemed restless. He hopped off a large leather couch and headed to an old desk that sat in the corner of the room. From here he produced a pack of playing cards and turned with a wicked smile… twenty minutes later and I was sat stark bollock naked with my hands cupping my Hampton. After a string of very bad cards that had been purposefully generated by Gio there seemed to be only yours truly fully unclothed. Not for long though; within the hour I found myself surrounded by a swarm of naked and playful women.

Gio was sat in a throne-like chair with a plump purple cushion placed between his legs. One of the larger Russians had decided to use a lampshade and was sat directly facing me. Unfortunately, the lampshade's narrower end gave me full sight of his slug-like, hairy penis. I moved seats.

So now I was sat next to a drop-dead doll who was wearing nothing but her underwear and an innocent face. She was part of the Russian contingent, but my language skills had been honed over the years.

'You are a proper fuckin beautski,' I slurred.

She looked back and said: 'Are you rich? What is your living?' in a heavily accented Russian purr.

Jesus H. Cut straight to the point why don't you? I gave it some thought and decided that it wasn't as if I was after a long-term relationship so it wouldn't hurt to overlook the shallowness of it all, at least until the morning.

'I work as a male model in Manchester city centre,' I almost automatically fired back.

She shook her beautiful little head and slowly sighed. 'And what is it you are modelling? Balaclavas?'

It seemed that we wouldn't be having a short-term relationship either.

So, after a lonely but comfortable night's sleep courtesy of Mr Jack Daniels I woke the following morning to the shrill call of a distant telephone. The noise echoed around Gio's house but not enough for someone to actually answer it. I hauled myself from the bed and pulled myself together to go in search. I was most definitely suffering. As I walked from room to room the crescendo rose as the phone neared and my head pounded harder. Finally, I located the source and yanked the receiver from the cradle.

'Hello!' I shouted rather angrily down the line.

A pause, and then a male voice. 'Who is this?'

'It's the Bigun and he's not very happy. Do you know what time it is?'

'Yes. Time for you to go and get Giorgio. Now. Tell him his Chairman needs a word.'

Shit. It was Franny Lee, the Manchester City Chairman. I should have recognised his voice, but my faculties were failing me.

'I'll go and fetch him for you now. I think he's just come in from a run.'

With a throbbing head and a parched mouth, I hurtled up the stairs and threw Gio's bedroom door open.

'Oi, you midget, you lazy fuckin gypsy, Franny Lee's on the phone for you downstairs.'

The lump of duvet in the middle of the large bed did not stir. I leaned over and grabbed the corner of the cover and yanked. Lying under the cover (fully clothed, I hasten to add) were both Gio and Nicky Summerbee. As they both woke, I couldn't help but break into laughter.

'You look beautiful together in bed, boys,' I wheezed out. I know Nicky wasn't around when I'd left the previous night's proceedings, so I guess he arrived after I'd retired to my cot.

'Fuck off Bigun,' came back his tired and short reply, 'and do not tell Francis I was here!'

Nicky pulled the cover back over himself as Gio rolled out of the bed and looked at me. His eyes were rolling and when he opened his mouth all he could emit was a dry growl.

'T'k'ven didi makhinji ox.'

Now I knew Gio really wasn't happy. He would always revert to his home tongue when truly miffed; which was alright by me as any offending remarks went right over my head.

The following day Gio was outside my house. It was a little after ten and the dull grey of a Mancunian morning sky didn't add to my mood. I hauled myself out of my bed and headed down the stairs to let him in.

He was through the door in a flash, all hurried and flustered. 'C'mon you big, lazy ape. You get ready.'

'Morning, Gio. How are you?' came my reply.

Gio paused and after a realisation came his apologetic clipped English.

'I'm sorry, Paul. You are more of a bear than an ape in the mornings.'

I laughed and pulled him into a headlock. As usual Gio gripped the inside of my thigh and twisted my flesh powerfully. I howled out and then lifted Gio off the floor so he was upside down in my hallway. I looked out the still open front door and hoped that no one would pass. Not sure what they'd make of the large man in underpants dangling Manchester City's star player.

After dusting ourselves down Gio informed me that he'd not heard from Demetrio and wanted to visit him and make sure he was well after the death of his mother.

I quickly threw some clobber on and hopped into his Ferrari and we fired off through Levenshulme, drawing looks from most due to the jet plane roar the car was making. We finally arrived at the restaurant and glided to a halt outside.

The front of the restaurant had a distinctly new look. Gone were the large windows, replaced by large pieces of plywood, and the entrance to the property also had a nice new grey steel gate surround. Gio sat in the driving seat with his mouth wide open. He removed his sunglasses, hoping his initial view had been distorted. It hadn't. The restaurant was still fully boarded up.

'What the fuck is this?' Gio was now facing me and looking confused.

'This is a boarded-up bistro Gio, and a goodbye to that money you lent him as well.'

I could quite easily throw in 'I told you so' but that would serve to help nobody at all.

From that moment Gio was a different man. It wasn't the outstanding money that had lit the fire of obsession in him, it was more the disrespect and breakage of trust. Each and every day I'd receive a phone call or text message in which he'd lambast Demetrio and his dirty deed. Finally, when I could take no more, I told Gio that I would endeavour to use all my worldly contacts to try and locate the errant Italian.

I asked Gio what I should do if I actually managed to lay hands on him.

'You're to tell him how disappointed I am, and you're also going to get me my money back.'

Fair enough.

'You can keep a grand as well, for your troubles.'

Once again, fair enough.

So, I put my feelers out around town and tracked down a 'guy that knew a guy'. He was also Italian and knew him well. He explained that it was no secret, amongst those that knew, that Demetrio had a gargantuan gambling problem. Huge, he explained. He had debts up to his eyeballs and had been gambling with Gio's money!

The informant explained that Demetrio frequented one place in town, a casino. If he was anywhere, then that would be the best place to track him down, he said. Well, I knew what the dodgy bastard looked like, so I took it upon myself to go after him. I went into the casino the guy mentioned, scouted about and asked a few faces; but had no joy. So I started going to all the casinos and gambling dens I could find. Eventually, after bandying Demetrio's name around enough, another guy said that he'd holed up in Birmingham and he kindly gave me the address. By now, Gio had upped the stakes in the same way that he did with the eating challenges and had said that if I got the money back, I'd get a couple of grand. Happy days.

Naturally, I got some muscle to come with me, and me and my big mate jumped in a car and hammered down to the address that I'd been given the very next day. I knocked on the door, with my equally big mate stood next to me, and waited, bristling with excitement and a bit of nerves. Eventually the door was answered. By a woman. We explained in as menacing a tone as you can use with a woman why we there and what we wanted to be leaving with. She kicked off. She went mental at us!

She was adamant that Demetrio, who she was married to or otherwise (we didn't ask), was no longer involved in that sort of thing. She wouldn't call him, and we didn't even know if he was there, but neither of us were the type to manhandle a woman, even if she was verbally tearing strips off us in the street. We decided to retreat and reassess what we needed to do, and returned to the car. As we did, a load of flashing blue lights and sirens hammered around the corner. She'd called the police on us!

We were arrested for harassment and driven down to the station, questioned and released after three hours. Fortunately, there were no charges filed against us; but it was a close one. Demetrio had found out that we were on to him and had said that we were harassing him and his family. Of course, as is so often the case in life, it had been a gentlemen's agreement between Gio and Demetrio, so we had no proof.

We had tried, and we had unfortunately failed. We knew the slimy little bastard had done a runner and he knew we knew. He could also have pressed charges against us, which was the last thing we needed; so, in the end, nothing came of it, but Georgi was grateful though.

Like I said, he is still loved very much in Manchester; and on his last visit we went to the hospital where Anthony Rowen was laid up terminally ill. One of his dying wishes was to meet his hero, Kinkladze. The lad's a proper Braveheart and has terminal multiple sclerosis. His sister got in touch with us, and with a few calls back and forth, we had arranged to go and meet him.

The meeting had been set up with a warning from his sister, and then the ward nurse, that he was so, so weak that they'd hardly had a peep out of him for days. We were told to expect little or no reaction, as sad as that was. What happened was very different to that. When we walked in, and Anthony saw who it was, his eyes lit up and he seemed to be temporarily filled with life. Then he lifted himself up and with great effort, in as strong a voice as his state could muster, he softly chanted, 'Gio, Gio, Gio.'

Gio was so touched, and with moist eyes we sat down and spoke with him for as long as he could maintain in his weak state.

He was a trooper though, and he made sure he got a good conversation with his hero. It makes the hairs go up on my arms thinking about that lad and that day.

It was funny, it was moving, and there wasn't a dry eye in that room.

Chapter Eleven
Reality Strikes

After the argument with Liam regarding the press I began to notice things were changing between me and the lads, although probably a little too late. Who knows, I could have turned things round, but by the time I'd clocked on to it, like I said, it was too late.

We were out on the town in London when I first noticed a real and tangible change in how the guys in the band were treating me. Oasis were playing at the Emporium, and so we had arranged to meet them there. It didn't matter how many times I'd seen them, I was proud of them, so I'd always watch them again and again. There was myself and my mate Geoff Bully. We had five quid in our pockets, and rocked up to the gig hoping to get a few drinks on the sly, as you do when you're a bit brassic.

It was still travelling at great expense and as I didn't have much money I'd take all I could get. Looking back it was blatantly obvious I wasn't as welcome as I had been, but sometimes it takes me a while!

So there we were after backstage laughs after the gig down south; we went on to a bar where things were a bit more back to how they had been. I was sat with Liam and we were catching up on what was going on. None of the others came to see me, and that hurt. Liam made some excuse for it, but they just didn't want anything to do with me at that point.

Still, Liam was there and no matter how the rest had changed, when Liam and me get together, it always goes back to how it was. It does now, and did back then, even when it was sour with everyone else. Even when all the legal stuff had just been kicking off and I saw him at the cricket ground, his first reaction was to talk to me, which shows what a nice bloke he is.

So at least we were normal; but nothing around us seemed to be. There was a woman walking around offering up a wicker basket of fruit to anyone who wanted it. I wondered what the hell it was; you didn't get this up north. She was very obviously off her tits, everyone was. That was when things took an even more surreal turn when Paul Yates marched up to where we were sat! I was sitting next to Liam and Bully was sat opposite me. We all watched and then realised what she was up to as she made a beeline for Liam.

It was like watching a lioness hunt her prey. Paula Yates: now she was a beautiful, vivacious woman. She was human Viagra, that girl; she seemed to ooze naughtiness from her every pore. When she took a shine to someone, she let it be known to anyone and everyone. Married or not. She went into flirt overdrive with Liam and he just did not know how to take it, bless him.

She lunged towards him. Liam flinched away with a cry of fear and said, 'You're only after the scandal, you are. My mum would kill me!' and then ran away. We all pissed ourselves laughing, when she just kind of shrugged her shoulders and swivelled round to smile at us.

I got her to sit with us a while, and she plonked herself down next to me and opposite Bully, very worse for wear but very happy. She also seemed to have forgotten her underwear, which Bully made it his duty to point out, literally. Finger pointed, he shouted, 'You've got no knickers on!'

She wasn't fazed one bit, just smiled and continued to cuddle up next to me. More women with more fruit approached with their wicker baskets, and it all just seemed a bit weird, but by now I didn't care. I didn't know what the hell was going on, especially when Paula started having a go at her mate who was one of the fruit basket carriers. Everyone was nuts! That was the 90s, I suppose.

Before long, Bully also decided to go for a wander, leaving me and the hot mess without knickers on alone. Well, dear reader, what could I do? She was very obviously warmed up, and I was human, so obviously thought she was gorgeous; so we began to get it on. Me and Paula Yates!

It was a great end to a night that had started off a bit dodgy. It left me with some good memories that may have been otherwise tarnished – so all good.

Ian Robertson, known as Rob, was security for Oasis for a few of the early years. He was ex forces and was a very nice guy. He just happened to be a very nice guy who didn't have the right personality for the job he was doing.

Forces people tend to be regimented. If they weren't, they wouldn't be very good in the forces. That's just how it works. I've no issues with that and I admire them for it. However, it's not a life for me, and it certainly isn't for a bunch of young lads on a meteoric rise who enjoy partying, late nights, girls, booze and drugs.

Ian Robertson wanted things compartmentalised. He wanted them tidy and organised and with everyone behaving. Rock and roll bands aren't there to behave! They're there to do the exact opposite.

So he'd be there, telling them off and telling their mates off (including me). Actually disciplining us all. Well, you can imagine what the reaction was each time.

There was one occasion when we'd all been to a gig with them playing. Afterwards, we were all sat in the bar of a hotel. I had Liam on one side and my mate Bully on the other, slumped in his chair, half asleep. This was at a time when it was all beginning to change and people were jumping on the Oasis bandwagon. There were crowds outside the hotel all wanting a glimpse of the lads and there were hangers on inside the hotel. We knew hardly any of them.

Anyway, this London bloke with a pony tail approached Liam and said something that wasn't actually meant to be antagonistic, but was actually quite intelligent. Liam obviously missed the point, got pissed off and started having a go at ME as if it was me that had said it.

Naturally I told him to do one, pointing out that I'd said nothing and to wind his neck in. Meanwhile, the Southern Pony Tail geezer was pissing himself laughing at what was happening in front of his eyes. I turned to Pony Tail and told HIM where to go, as he'd upset my mate who was now having a go at me.

'You're taking the fucking piss, mate,' he had the cheek to say back to me.

'You what? How am I taking the piss? I'm just sat here and YOU come over and take the piss.'

'It was you!'

'It was you, you cockney c..' Well, you can guess where it was going.

Liam then began to kick off, siding with London boy against me, and unsurprisingly, I was not having it. I mean, what the hell had just happened?! I was wound up by now, and a bit taken aback by the speed of this turn of events, but also at my best mate going a bit weird on me. I didn't get what was going on.

Now this was in the period when things were changing, and I wasn't in the best frame of mind anyway. I already felt like I was losing my mates, and could feel that I was being shut out. So it didn't take much to trigger me off.

So I fronted up to the guy with the pony tail. I still don't know who the hell he was. All of his mates who were with him stood up to back him up; and all I had was Bully who was sleeping in his chair, and Liam, who for some reason had turned against ME.

I was still ready to go though. I was still fully prepared to kick off and sort this lot out. I would not back down, because I'm a Viking and I felt like I was being picked on, by London, by the music industry which was taking my mates and turning my dream into something totally different.

So while I was there, assessing who to go for, what chairs could be thrown, assessing things like Robocop, big Forces Rob sidled up to me.

'Bigun, can you pipe down, mate?'

'WHAT?' I snapped back.

'Can you calm down, there's too many of them,' he said. He was quite obviously shitting himself at the number of people there, which I didn't care about one bit. But my red mist was abating. I was calming down despite the numb nuts around me.

I walked away, mumbling, fuming, and went to the toilets to calm myself down. The sensible thing to do. Next thing I knew, Rob walked in and came up to me. He was looking me dead in the eye and he said, 'Bigun. I understand.'

'Do what?' I said. 'Don't you come in here patronising me. You don't know nothing mate. You're meant to be looking the lads, get out there and look after the people you're paid to look after.'

I was in a rage again, and I needed him to step away from me. I see now that he was actually being a decent bloke and was doing it right, but at the time I didn't see that. I saw something - someone - that I wanted to kick and punch, to take my frustrations out on.

I mean, we are talking hangers on here, many of them, and Liam couldn't see it. It was all happening so fast and it felt out of my control. Liam didn't see it then, but he did eventually. He knows what's what that lad, but then, he was young, and his head was turned. So much of the bullshit that was to come could've been avoided if we'd got past that, if he'd seen what was happening; but at the time he didn't. And I didn't have the maturity that I do now to articulate it to him.

If it was me and him as we are now, it never would've gone the way it did. But it did. It was part of the start of the end. They'd changed, and it was becoming blatantly obvious (even to me) that I wasn't as welcome as I had been, even though I'd kicked it all off for them.

It was sad. It really wrenched at my heart each time things like this got through to me. I see the world with rose tinted glasses, anyone who knows me would tell you that. So because of that, it probably took longer for me to catch on than it would most people.

I always loved those lads though, even when we were falling out. I always did and I always will, no matter what happens; cos I'm the Bigun and got them together so they could change the world.

Chapter Twelve
Time Waits for no Man

The original Oasis drummer, Tony McCarroll, is a sound geezer, or a Spartan as he likes to put it in his book *Oasis - The Truth*. When he went through the mill when he was unceremoniously dumped from Oasis, I always tried to be there for him.

It's no secret and is already out there that he was duped by a contract several inches thick that his name had been added to as an afterthought in pen, and resulted in him being ousted from Oasis. It hit him hard and rightly so. I felt bloody sorry for the guy. Ultimately, he got some due payment when the band forced him to take legal action. You know they even appealed against the Musician's Union representing him. Kick a man while he's down why don't you? I guess you don't just forget all of that overnight. Not when your input into making musical history lives forever and is echoed in the choruses that you played drums over. That's a lot to weigh on your mind, that is.

Fair play to Tony though, as he always stood up to Noel when he thought he was doing things that were untoward, but it's just a damn shame that he was duped by the band's solicitor. It's always easy to be wise after the event, and I can testify to that!

Me and Tony both felt the sharp end of dealing with Oasis, and you could certainly say that we shared a dark period together, but above all he was there for me when I was on my arse and needed to get back on my feet after my first court case went tits up. I was there for him when he got sacked from Oasis, especially as I just lived around the corner. He was there for me twice when my car valeting business needed a boost when I had been sacked by Oasis (or at least felt like I had).

Three or four years had passed and I'd been doing my best to get everything back on track, and I'm pleased to say that throughout we'd remained solid friends, me and Tony. When he got paid up originally with some money from royalties one of the first things he did was to plough some cash into my car valeting business to get it back up and running again.

He knew I'd had it a bit rough, and he asked if I wanted to get back into it and earn an honest crust, which of course I did.

He just turned up one morning saying that he wanted to buy a new car and did I know of anyone. I said that I knew a kid at City who had a nice motor for sale. That kid happened to be Gary Mason. So we went down there, and all the time he was obviously sounding me out. He liked it when we got there; it was a lovely black Beemer so he was chuffed.

Next thing I knew he said 'Bigun, did you want to get back into the valeting, as I can help you out and get you a van. I can get you all the gear and you can get properly back on your feet mate.'

I was gobsmacked. I mean, what a guy. I knew we were mates, but that was above and beyond the call of any duty of any mate. And of course, I wasn't gonna say no to him, so I pretty much bit his hand off.

So after we bought that car from Gary Mason down at Manchester City we added a van to the shopping list, and then all of the equipment needed to get me back into my valeting business. I was good to go.

Six months had passed, and thanks to Tony Mc I had the van, the equipment and a bit of self-respect back, and I'd been out and won all my old contracts back too. Things were rocking and rolling again. Happy days. Little did I know that things were going to take another nasty turn.

I'd got Manchester City back as one of those contracts, but at the time the Council were being funny about parking and cleaning cars in Platt Lane, so I had to park the van out on the street and clean cars out on the road. It was ridiculous, but we'd got round it, but it had obviously drawn the eye of some thieving bastards.

There I was one day, me and my mate cleaning one of the footballers' lovely cars out on the road, working out of the back of the van with all the new gear in, and next thing we knew, the bloody van roared off.

Me and my mate looked at each other with chamois leathers in hands, staring at each other with mouths agape over the car we were cleaning. Then it twigged. Some little bastard had nicked it!

When the van hurtled off, the doors were open and about three grands' worth of stuff fell out onto the road, the pressure washer, the products; they all scattered everywhere. Somehow the 25 litre barrel of water in the back of the van had also burst, after falling over, and that was pissing everywhere out the back of the van as it careered down the road.

Next thing we knew, as we stared at the van disappearing down the road, Nicky Summerbee pulled up in his car alongside us.

'What's going on lads?' he asked, not really needing to: 'Get in the car, we'll get them.' Legend.

'Follow that water!' I shouted, pointing at the trail leading away into the distance.

So Summerbee floored the motor and we followed the watery trail. Before you know it we were being led through the streets of Moss Side, weaving in and out of the streets, following the path of the van. The mongrels must've cottoned on to the fact that they were giving away their route, and pulled over and left the van in the middle of the road and took the bloody keys with them. Little shites.

It took ages to get that van back, new keys sorted, new ignition, the alarm sorted and all of that. A few weeks later, I walked out of my house and saw a couple of sponges hanging out the back of the same van. The little scrotes had bided their time and come back, with the keys that still worked somehow, and nicked all the equipment that had fallen out the first time. I was raging!

That was even in the paper, that little escapade. Something along the lines of 'Nicky Summerbee saves the day'.

So there I was back at virtually square one. I had the van, I had the contacts, but some little oiks had all the equipment I needed to carry on. And do you know what? The legend, the Spartan that is Tony McCarroll, bailed me out AGAIN. He's the soundest bloke, he is. I wouldn't be where I am today were it not for him.

I always tried to be there for him when he was in the doldrums. We'd fanny about, going here and there, and sometimes went to see football matches with a bunch of the lads.

Big Mark, or 'Mark Tasty' as I like to call him, comes up a lot in my stories, and I'm not lying when I say that he's like my giant Viking Guardian Angel. He also had Tony's back when he was with him.

There was this one time when there was me, Big Mark and my mate Jason Watson, all at a Manchester City game with Tony, in the old stadium at Maine Road. These were the days before all the money was chucked at it like it is these days.

Oasis had always loved their football. We all did. Like anyone in Manchester, in fact. It's well documented that in Manchester people fall in to two camps: red or blue. In our little group we were a mix of Blues and Reds supporters, but this day was about City. Because the money was coming in now, Oasis were always being photographed in the VIP boxes at football matches, and nowhere more so than at the Man City games.

You would have no doubt seen the legendary gig they did there in 1996, that's out there amongst the most legendary gigs. So it held a special place in their hearts and their history. Manchester. Football. Maine Road. Oasis. It was a magical place with a magical history.

Tony was dealing with it all ok, considering what had happened. But we weren't there for that. And besides, with the constant sniping he got, he had a thick skin to an extent as long as there was a bit of distance between him and them.

There we were sat, happily watching everything, until I saw that it was actually Noel coming up the stairs towards where we were sat. I nudged Tony, nodded towards Brezhnev (as I call him) and said, 'Isn't that Noel?' in as conversational a tone as I could muster.

So there went the distance. Poor Tony, this was at a time when everything was raw and before the court case when he finally got a bit of closure. Well, it obviously affected him as he started shaking like a leaf. I think it was part anger, part adrenaline, and here was the cause of all his recent obsessions since being kicked out of Oasis. And he was coming up to where we were. For all we knew Noel was coming to have a word, and I think that's what really made Tony go like that. You would think that, wouldn't you?

I said to him that he shouldn't do anything, which is, of course, rich coming from me, I know. He said that he must, as he wasn't sure he'd get another chance. Like I said, this was before he got his chance through the courts and got to have his say.

So Noel continued to walk up the stairs, Tony sat stone faced, and then it was as if everyone in the stadium held their breath... and... he walked straight past us. He must have adopted that thing that famous people do when they're out in public, where they purposely don't focus on anything or anyone around them for fear of catching a manic fan's eye and getting stuck talking for half an hour. I genuinely don't believe he ignored us on purpose. He walked right past and then on into the tunnel that then led into the inner part of the stadium.

Of course, we all sighed with relief. I looked up and realised immediately where he was going, as I could clearly see Liam in a VIP box that would be accessed from inside the stadium, where Noel had just entered. I knew Tony wanted to do something, anything; and I wanted to do something, but there was no way we were going up there. Not me or Tony. We knew we'd never get past anyone on the door. With this Tony departed.

Big Mark then said: 'I can go up there if you want, and have a word.' What a man, I thought, and further suggested to Jason that he went up with him and gave them shit with him.

I watched them bowl up the stairs and then disappear into the tunnel, and of course we had to be told of what happened between then and when they came back to our seats.

Apparently, they got up to the box unchallenged, and Jason went in and started having a go immediately.

'You're out of order you lot are, what you've done to my pal,' he said, pointing at Noel and Liam and anyone else within pointing range.

So obviously all hell broke loose among the assembled glitterati, and Noel pointed out Jason and Mark to his security guards who then grabbed hold of them and threw them down the stairs. There was no damage done, not to the guys at least, but there was to the bar up in the box. Or at least some of the stock of liquid up there.

It turned out that when it all kicked off and Brezhnev ordered his muscle to evict these sayers of truth, one of them managed to swipe a big bottle of Jack Daniels and secrete it in their coat whilst in there.

So, a few minutes had passed, and then Big Mark and Jay came back to our seats and explained what had happened and produced the bottle of JD. Of course, after the forced exit, all of them in the box, including Noel and Liam, were peering down to watch where they were going to, so they would have seen them reach us and then collude. As soon as I looked up I saw Liam looking back at me, who then proceeded to give his famous two fingers up to me. So I responded to his two fingered salute in a similar fashion, and then held the bottle of Jack Daniels aloft with a hearty 'fuck you' to boot. Liam clocked the bottle and realised what had happened and renewed his two fingered response with greater gusto. He was smiling when he did it, I'm sure he was. I mean, what had happened? Words said and a bottle nicked. They didn't send anyone after the bottle anyway.

We were all pissing ourselves now and swigging from the bottle, showing off and revelling in this little victory. It cheered Tony up no end, and made a football match even more interesting than it already was.

You should read that man's book, if you haven't done so already. I'm fine with that now that you've bought mine! Check it out, it's *Oasis - The Truth* and it's by the man, the legend, the Oasis drummer and friend of mine, Mr Tony McCarroll.

Chapter Thirteen
My Mate, Goldenbollocks

If there's a name of a footballer that's bigger than just sport and football itself and is known the whole world over, it's Mr. David Beckham. He's a fashion icon, he's a dad, he's a philanthropist, he's an all-round nice bloke; women want him and men want to be him, but above all, he is a bloody good footballer. He's rich as a bastard and cool as you like.

David Robert Joseph Beckham OBE played for Manchester United, Preston North End, Real Madrid, Milan, Los Angeles Galaxy, Paris Saint-Germain, and the England national team. He was the first English player to win league titles in four countries, England, Spain, the United States and France. After 20 years of playing, he finally retired on 18 May 2013, after playing his final emotional game.

It was with Manchester United that his glittering career started, where he made his first-team debut in 1992 aged 17. Both of his parents, and subsequently he, were massive Manchester United fans. It was therefore bloody huge for them all when his fame exploded and he became forever heralded as part of the 'Class of 92'. It was just before this period in his life that I first met him and despite his fame and riches, he has remained the eternal gentleman that he was when I met him.

I was cleaning cars at the Manchester United grounds, in the very early days before it all kicked off between Fergie and me. This was before the band had taken off, and before Becks had started on his meteoric rise to super-fame. It must have been about 1991. Becks had just come back to Manchester United after a stint at Preston, and at that time Liam was off doing his things so he was beginning to no longer help me clean cars.

I have to say that as and when I met all of the lads that were to become the Class of '92 - Nicky Butt, Paul Scholes, Phil Neville, Gary Neville and Ryan Giggs - I got on well with them all. They were all really nice blokes. Beckham was beyond even that, he was good as gold, that man, and we became pretty good mates. I got on so well with him, it was like we had a connection from the moment we met.

Us meeting and getting to know each other happened at a time when he was seeing more and more money coming in as he became increasingly successful, but was only just starting with his cars. He had yet to get to the stage of going up the ranks motor-wise. He had just exchanged whatever he had at that time for Ryan Giggs' red Ford Escort. You'd never see that happen these days, with the amount of money that footballers see early doors in their careers. Now you see teenagers buying Ferraris, but this was a different time, and Becks wanted that red Ford Escort.

When he got it, I don't mind telling you that it was a total shithole. It was a state. Disgusting. I was the go-to man then for cars being done, so Beckham said to me, 'Just do what you can with it, Bigun.'

I tell you, dear reader, I had my work cut out. I must have spent five hours cleaning that grubby little car. FIVE BLOODY HOURS. That's how bad it was. I didn't have the equipment then, I didn't have the chemicals that you need. So I had to clean that dump of a car by hand with washing up liquid, a scrubbing brush and some good old-fashioned elbow grease. What with all of the equipment and lotions and potions that I have now today, with F1 Mobile Valeting, I could have got that car gleaming inside and out within an hour. This was the early days though, and I put my heart and soul into making Becks's new car look (and smell) lickety spit!

Obviously, I wanted to impress Beckham, so I went all out to get it looking mint. There are things I was pulling out of that car that Ryan Giggs left in there that I can't even tell you. It was a disgusting job, but I did it. So when Becks came out after training, he was blown away with what I'd done. He was so, so pleased that he had me do his cars for years, even kept me on after that unfortunate incident when Fergie kicked me out. All that changed when that happened was that I went to his house to clean his motors instead of the training grounds. Those cars went up and up in value, but he never really changed. That was the moment I got his respect, anyway; and he always had mine and still does to this day.

There was always a link between Becks, Liam and me. Obviously Liam met Becks through me and the valet business, and then it was partly the football, but mostly that it seemed that they were both sprinkled with magic dust around the same time. Becks always loved Oasis too, and even copied Liam's hair at one point. That just shows how long ago this was. These days, David wears something or does something and the whole world follows. Back then, he copied the hair of my best mate!

Then of course there was a time when I was going through all the legal crap with the band and things weren't that great in my life. I loved the lads, I always have and I always will; but they weren't my favourites at the time. You know like you can be with family? Well that's how it was then. I loved them to the bone but was ready to rumble with them at a moment's notice! Maybe I had an empty space to fill, where my mates had been but were now elsewhere, and I got from Becks something that filled that void a bit. I dunno, but maybe that was it at the time.

So I went to Beckham's house one time in that period and he opened the door to show me how much he really did like Oasis - there he stood with the same hair as Liam! It was when they did Glastonbury, around the turn of the millennium and everyone was all over it. Liam had famously just cut off all of his shaggy hair, and there was Becks stood in front of me having done the same. I didn't know how to react! I mean, he was copying the guy who had been my best mate but who I was also trying to sue at that point in time. Well, I was there to wash Mr. OCD's car so that he could go see Oasis play at The Apollo in Manchester. Fate can be a cruel mistress.

When I was done, he came out to the car wearing a fishtail parka as well as the same hair as LG and my jaw dropped. It was weird.

I said, 'David, are you trying trip me out here, or what?'

'Whaddaya mean, Bigun?' he asked.

'Mate, you're dressed like my old best mate who I'm taking to court!' I wailed back.

He just grinned that grin, climbed in his gleaming car and off he went. Little did he know how much he was going to get the piss ripped out of him that night. The band were giving it large up on stage and Liam saw Becks down the front, dressed like he would and with the same hair. Needless to say, he started pointed at him and abusing him in front of the crowd, all in good humour, of course. Becks tried to hide from it all, but in typical Liam style he involved the crowd, telling them that Becks was there with his haircut, and the piss taking ensued on an even grander scale.

Of course, Becks was as popular as Lima in Manchester then, despite Blues and Reds rivalry, so it was all done with the best humour and tongue in cheek, like.

As I said, it was before then, around the time the band were on the brink of big success, that coincided with the time when I first really got to know Beckham. It must have been around '91 to '92, just before he himself went super famous. So while Oasis were really taking off and I was seeing less and less of the lads, I kind of latched on to Becks. Not in any kind of sad way. I looked up to the guy; I mean, who doesn't? I was going to his house five or six times a week after Fergie kicked me out. David knew what had happened and he also knew what had happened with Oasis as well. Bless his heart, he didn't have to stick with me; but he did. I was up there most of the week. He had a lot of cars after a while, but it's also no secret that he is a bit OCD when it comes to cleanliness, and that extends to his fleet of cars. He likes them clean. All the time. So, he put that business my way, that's the kind of gent that he was and remains to this day.

I truly believe that part of David Beckham's astounding success is down to how much of a nice man he is. That, and the magic dust sprinkled on him! He has integrity and he has respect for everybody. He doesn't look down on those that others would perceive as below them. I've seen a number of people, including footballers, turn into monsters once fame and fortune knocks on their door. Not Becks. Not a chance.

The trust he had in me grew, and as a result there were times when I provided a service that went beyond valeting his cars. It was an honour to do so, and it was gratefully received in a period when things could've been going better in my personal life.

There was one particular period around the time of the World Cup when the press were being particularly intrusive to Becks and his family. *The Sun* were camped outside with a cake to give him to say 'get well' as he'd got recently injured. He wanted to escape his own house without the reporters and paparazzi all jumping on his car as he left.

He called me and said, 'Paul, I've just bought myself a Rolls Royce Phantom, but the one they've given me is a loan car. I don't want to be followed in it; can you come over and help me out giving the paps the runaround?'

Of course, I was right on that and I told him so.

At this time, he had his foot in plaster. The injury was a broken fibula which he'd managed to do in a full on tackle during a Champions League match that Manchester United won against Spanish team Deportivo La Coruna. It was seven weeks before the World Cup and England had qualified purely through Beckham's last-minute free-kick against Greece. They reckoned he'd need eight weeks to recover, so naturally the press were all over it.

Anyone who doesn't live in this sceptered isle of ours can't fully comprehend what the British press are like. They love to build things up to smash them down to the ground. When the World Cup approaches, this goes into overdrive. The hysteria is ridiculous leading up to it, and the pressure that is piled on our teams is huge. Once our teams don't perform, it turns into a witch hunt and a different kind of hysteria altogether. It turns nasty.

So when I rocked up to Posh and Becks' house, the media circus that they are always subjected to was at a level much higher than normal. We had qualified. We had qualified because of their beloved Becks, who was a constant target of their focus. All hopes were pinned on him, and then he broke a bone. They were like starving dogs locked down and held at bay in front of a butchers.

I eased through them, parked up and went inside the house, where the noise of the assembled press was temporarily muffled. Posh was there with Brooklyn and her sister, and the hairdresser was there too, and of course, there was David Beckham, anxiously wanting to escape the house and the clutches of the baying media. We planned and plotted and finally exited the house out of sight of the cameras. I jumped in the Roller with the hairdresser, and Beck jumped into his Navigator/Escalade with Posh, her sister and Brooklyn; and off we sped. We went through the gates, me first in the Rolls Royce and the Escalade/Navigator behind, the camera flashes popped and strobed around us, and the shouts of the press were muted thankfully by the Roller's build quality. I felt like a star. That said, it was pretty scary and full on. They deal with that sort of attention day in and day out, and I don't envy them that.

We shot out, turned left, turned left again and within seconds we were at the top of a road and parked up; we climbed out ready to do the planned swap. I could see down the road that a Mercedes was on our trail and was presumably full of press. Posh ran up to me. She didn't have any make-up on and was hardly recognisable. She was clearly upset and buried her head in my chest.

'Get rid of them, Paul. I'm sick of this.' Her attentions then turned on Beckham: 'You and your bloody cars, David. I've had enough of it!'

Becks just grinned and beckoned Posh over and they all climbed into the Rolls Royce Phantom and roared off away from all of the hassle. I watched them hammer off, and then jumped into the big gleaming Navigator and headed back towards the house, where all the press were. As far as anyone watching, including the press, was concerned, someone, probably the Beckhams, had just left in the car I was now in and here it was coming back up to re-enter the house! Or so they thought.

I pulled up and stopped by them, instead of going back into the house as they expected, and they swarmed around me as I drew up alongside them. Then a woman knocked on my tinted window, babbling away and telling me that she wanted to give me a cake. Or rather she wanted to give Beckham a cake, but the tint on the windows and the power of assumption stopped her realising who it was. So I looked at the big old cake from *The Sun*, wishing Beckham well on the healing of his fibula, and broke out in a massive grin.

I pressed a button and wound down the window, grabbed it off her, thanked her very much to her shocked face; and drove off home, where we all had a bit of Becks's cake. The look on her face when it dawned on her that she was handing the cake over to a total stranger was priceless!

The next day, he called me back round to both bring back and clean the car, as he was going to a do what I seem to remember was 'Player of the Year' and he wanted to arrive in spick and span style.

When I got there, I parked up, left the keys in the ignition and closed the door. The door locked! I couldn't bloody believe it.

My heart sank and I broke out in a cold sweat. Then I saw that luck may just have been on my side, after all. The window was open just a crack. I had to get back in that car!

I looked around, exasperated, and then I looked up and saw that Becks was watching me from an upstairs window.

'What the bloody hell have you done, Paul?' he shouted down. He wasn't even angry. But I was so embarrassed! I asked him to chuck down a coat hanger, which he did. So, both he and Posh were hanging out of the window watching me for an hour and a half, laughing at me and taking the piss, as I tried to gently break in to this car. The stress I went through, feeling so bloody silly and knowing that they were watching me the whole time! I was ill with it!

While I tried to physically get into it, I also had his car agent on the phone trying to get the number for the key pad which was the alternative entry method. He didn't have it, and Becks was beginning to stress as he needed to get to the do, and his other car at the time, the new Roller, hadn't been delivered yet. Finally, I managed to break in with the help of the coat hanger. And what a relief it was when that door opened. Posh and Becks cheered from their front row seats, the window upstairs, and I sighed the biggest sigh of relief. I was buzzing.

Fortunately, when I apologised, Becks just said not to worry about it, and that it was his fault as he should have the spare keys and didn't. What a nice guy. I did feel a bloody fool, though.

It was in 2008, years later, having not seen him for a while as he'd been here there and everywhere, when I heard from him for the first time in ages. My phone went off with a number I didn't recognise. That wasn't unusual, so I answered. It was Becks, and he was at The Lowry for the Spice Girls reunion, and while he was there he wanted his car made beautiful by yours truly. So down I went, and he came out with the keys to whatever car it was at that time and gave me a hug.

'How do fancy going to see the Spice Girls tonight?' he asked me, catching me off guard.

'Oh, erm, yes, the girls would love that,' I said, knowing that my daughters would love it. I didn't have the heart to say that I'd bloody hate it, but it was right up their street. So down came Becks's agent with a handful of tickets and he took my details for the guest list. I cleaned the car, we said our farewells and nice-to-see-you's and off I went home to give my daughters the good news. They were over the moon.

Later that night, we rocked up to the venue, I handed my tickets in and got led with my daughters into the hall. The usher pointed at the front row and explained that they were our seats! We were pretty much on the bloody stage. Needless to say, my girls were in bits, and I'd probably gone as pale as milk. I was at a Spice Girls concert, with two little girls, and I was in the front row. My street cred was not ready for this kind of hammering. What had I done? Time to keep a low profile, I thought to myself. No chance.

When they finally came on stage to 'Spice Up Your Life', there were lights, explosions and tens of thousands of people screaming and cheering. What did Posh do? Of course, she immediately clocked me trying to hide in the front row. Me, Mr. Oasis, still trying to look cool with a little girl either side of me and 'Spice Up Your Life' blaring out all around me. She was loving it, and probably nearly pissed herself as she was laughing so hard!

There were gays dancing all around me, the girls were in stitches and Posh was on stage laughing and pointing at me, gesturing for me, Mr. Oasis, to get up and dance with everybody. She knew how embarrassed I was, but fair play to her. Not my coolest moment, dear readers, I can tell you. I had to go to the bar and calm my nerves; there I was, going back and forth getting brandy after brandy.

When the whole challenging experience drew to a close, I saw Becks down the opposite side to me also at the front of the stage in a VIP section. Naturally, I got the girls to follow me and I went over to say hello to him and thank him for being part of organising the mammoth piss take that had just happened. As I drew nearer to him, massive security guards jumped in my path.

'What do you think you're doing?' the gorillas growled, menacingly.

'No, no, he's fine, let him in!' Becks shouted over, and they parted like a hairy Red Sea in front of me.

Well, the girls thought their dad was supercool when that happened. He was laughing at the look on my face and asked if I'd enjoyed the show, to which I replied with a lie, saying what a great experience it'd been. He pissed himself laughing, as he'd seen exactly how much I'd enjoyed it, which was not one bit!

Over the years, he was a very generous guy and he's looked after me in times that were dark, and that's all I'll say on the matter. He was instrumental in getting me through lows like when Fergie kicked me out and for that I'm eternally grateful. I have a picture I took of him on my wall and a hat trick football that he signed in my house to this day. I treasure that ball as it was one that Paul Scholes kicked into the crowd after a hat trick, and no one has those bad boys. My cousin's mate nabbed it instantly and ran off with it. I said to Becks that I'd wanted it and it had gone missing, and he said that he'd see what he could do, if he could track it down as it were. Next thing I knew, he called me and told me to get around there.

When I did, he handed this ball to me. I was over the moon, let me tell you. Not only was it signed by David Beckham, but there are little squiggles all over it as well. They're Brooklyn's attempts at autographs before he even had a handle on what autographs were! And there, across the main part of it are the words 'Congratulations from David Beckham.'

He didn't have to do that for me, but he did; and that sums up David Beckham.

Chapter Fourteen
Most Rock n Roll Legal Aid Ever

We all have our ups and downs in life. Every dog has his day. All of that. Whatever the influencing factors there are that cause it are subjective to the individual. Mine have been particularly low, but if you fast forward to now, everything is properly positive in my life and I couldn't be happier.

However, there's a path that took me to where I am now, and I don't want to shy away from the shit stuff. So, we now need to talk about some of that shit stuff, caused by a myriad of different things happening and circumstances being what they were, mixed with paths crossing at what was possibly the worst, or best, time for them to cross, depending upon who you speak to about it.

A particularly low time for me was when I took Oasis to court. Actually, let's not polish a turd. That was a really fucking low point in my life. I was on the bones of my arse, I felt muted. I was broken.

My mates that I'd grown up with, associated with, and put the dreams together with, had left me.

It felt to me like they'd ridden off on the crest of a wave, to global approval and domination; while I was left with nothing, but still literally answering the questions when I was walking down the street and trying to smile whilst doing it. It was tough. I found myself lying to save face, to make it look like they were still in touch with me and I was still an integral part of things. I mean, I'd had such a massive part to play in it all and they'd just wandered away from me saying I no longer had a purpose.

So there I was, as skint as a bastard, and I happened to meet Chris Carnell, who at that time was an up and coming agent who was sniffing round Georgi Kinkladze.

I was round Gio's house, at a time when he was thinking of transferring to Ajax or Liverpool. So there was this guy this particular night; he'd managed to wheedle his way in with Georgi. As he was an up and coming sports agent/solicitor, it was obvious why he was sniffing round Gio: he was trying to kick some doors in. I'm all for that; whatever your background, you have to kick doors in to get on in life. But you don't screw people over. That, ladies and gentlemen, I am not fine with.

So he turned up, all fancy clothes and car, looking the part and playing the part before he even WAS the part.

Georgi said to him: 'This is Paul, he put Oasis together.' As you'd expect from such a big statement, it got a big reaction. I can see it all now with the luxury of hindsight, but obviously, he latched onto me.

Gio then said to me: 'Tell him about what's happened.'

So I did. All of it.

Next thing I know, this guy said, 'You've got a case there, Paul.'

Now I didn't haven't a clue at the time what he was up to. But at this stage I was trying to think with my head and not my heart. I saw a glimmer of hope in an otherwise dark place and I reached for it.

It transpired that it wasn't just Noel who had a master plan. For his own reasons, this Chris bloke reeled me in. Whether I won or lost, he really didn't give a flying fuck, I now know. He said all this bollocks about word of mouth and that it's a breach of verbal contract.

Like a fish on a hook I said, 'Is it?' and he said that yes, I had a massive case and to come into his office, which I did one gloomy Wednesday morning to go through everything, and to put it all down in writing on a load of forms. It took ages, as anyone who's heard me telling my stories knows, but we got there.

So the first thing this man said after the last bit of information had been wrung out of me was, 'We're going to have to get you legal aid.'

My jaw hit the floor.

'Seriously? Who's going to give me legal aid to take the biggest band in the world to court?' I responded, incredulous.

But, incredibly, he explained how to do it and yes, I applied for legal aid to take the biggest band in the world at the time to court.

Now here's the thing that I always think about. There was a grey man somewhere out there sat behind a grey desk, in a grey suit, deciding to sign things off or deny things when it came to legal aid. Like I said, I didn't have a pot to piss in at the time, I'd fallen off the wave, so there was no way I could afford to pay any legal costs. Not a chance. So a pile of forms would have landed on his grey desk, he would have read them with his grey eyes and I like to imagine two grey eyebrows raising at the names on those forms. I like to think it brightened up his grey existence – and I thank him for it.

He must've been a Blur fan, that's all I can say. It took a further six months of fighting and form filling and working up the chain; but we did it. That man in the grey suit behind the desk where they say yes or no, he looked at my case and thought, 'This boy's been shafted here.' He signed it off! He signed off legal aid to take Oasis to court.

I couldn't believe it, but it was a much needed spark of hope for me at the time. The morning that envelope came through and I opened it to the news that it had been granted, well, I couldn't catch a breath. Not before or after.

I can only imagine what it must have been like the other end when Noel, Liam, Guigsy, Bonehead and Tony Mc opened their envelopes. They must have thought: 'That miserable bastard!' And why wouldn't they; they had lost touch with the real world, where I was left in it.

And so the slow legal wheels began to turn.

To reiterate: I still didn't want to do it, I missed my boys and I missed the band; but at the time I was convinced, partly by me and partly by Cornell, that it was my last and only chance. What else could I do?

At that time, I wasn't in a good place. What started it all was that me and Liam had fallen out because he'd promised me monies and they never came. I was going to gigs and he was giving it the big 'I am'. And, well, I just couldn't wear it. It was horrible seeing this man, who was the closest person to me in the band, drifting away from me, and to make it worse, drifting towards hangers-on.

I'm not saying I wanted him to take me with him, but he just wasn't being right. It was going to his head, and I could see it, do you know what I mean? I was seeing people round him, people who weren't genuine, and I'd point this out to him. I'd tell him they were knob'eads.

He didn't like it. So all of a sudden, that grip that we had with each other was breaking. It was sad. You see, I think if I'd have stayed with Liam, things would have been a lot smoother. It would've been a less bumpy ride. He wouldn't have needed all those idiots around him. I don't mean the band, I mean the plastic people who were always gathered around him. I felt like I'd become that person who had done his job and now was no longer needed. I no longer had a purpose. I was as good as discarded. I was superfluous to requirements.

Give him his due, Noel used to actually say to me, 'You need to get hold of something, you do, here. You need a purpose, now. You've done your job, you need to do something now, like doing Tony's drum kit or something.' He was always straight, Noel was.

'I can't do that,' I'd tell him. 'I can't be arsed with that. I'm a promoter, I'm a dream maker.' That's how I felt. I can't weave dreams when I'm sorting out a drum kit!

But it became a bit like that, it felt like I was just there, I no longer had a meaning. So to an extent, Noel was right. I could've stayed with them, but after two years, I could no longer keep my mouth shut. Early doors in that band, I'd had a lot of say. Now I was just hustling where I could to get some cash in. I wasn't getting anything back. I wasn't asking for it either, I want that to be known.

I didn't ask for any money, because I'd been promised money by Liam and I took him on his word.

So I hope you can see why I did what I did, this sorry arsed thing. Either way, it's water under the bridge now and this is how the whole sorry thing played out. I say sorry, but there was a very interesting thing happened the night beforehand with a very glamorous lady.

The court case was to be held in London at the High Court, so I went down south to London, to prepare for court. I went with a premier footballer who should probably remain nameless, but was there with me as moral support. He had ulterior motives being there, as he was seeing a woman in London called Melanie Sykes. She was a stunning yet arguably troubled model who had risen to fame through the Boddington's beer adverts.

We arranged to meet in Notting Hill with Mel and her mate at this swanky bar. Next thing I knew a geezer came over and introduced himself and who should it be? It was Des O'Connor's son, a guy called Finan. We all had a drink, and he turned out to be an absolute top lad. So before you know it all of us were getting merry together and it was going great.

The Footballer that shall not be named seemed to not be interested in Mel, like they'd lost their connection. I picked up on that and that she wasn't very happy. It turned out though that she seemed to be making a swerve for me, and even more surprising was that me and Mel got on pretty darn well. She was having a bit of a tough time then, and she seemed to be enjoying my company. The banter was going back and forth and we were having a right laugh. However, the Footballer didn't like it, and I could see he was getting a bit narked by it all.

Then O'Connor Junior piped up that he had an apartment, and we should all go back there. I wasn't sure about leaving the ambience of the bar when me and Mel were getting on so well, but it turned out to be above the bar we were in! This is awesome, that's what I was thinking.

We all bundled upstairs and this flat was mint. It was was in an L shape, done out beautifully and to a very high specification, and at the end of the L shape, it went round to a DJ booth and a dancefloor! It was amazing. Before you know it, the party started and I was having a bit of a bop with Mel Sykes. I was right into her by this time, and I noticed the Footballer was the other end chatting up Mel's friend now.

Next thing you know, things took a turn for the slobbery and passionate and I got a grip on Mel. It had all happened quickly and we were up against a wall and she was up for it and we were necking.

I was thinking: hang on, I'm in here!

I honestly could not believe it. My life had been so shitty for a while, and I was even taking my old pals to court the next day, but here I was snogging the beautiful Mel Sykes! It all went on for a while, just kissing and a bit of groping (well of course I did) but then the Footballer realised what was going on and he didn't like it one bit. His ego kicked in, and it seemed like a case of the Footballer not wanting to play with his football, but not wanting to allow anyone else to play with it either.

He made a point of being a bit of an arse and basically killed all joy in the room. We were unfortunately sharing a hotel room that night, me and the Footballer. So guess what? That was game over then and we went sulkily back to the hotel. He had the right arse, and it carried on when we got back there. That said, I had an important day the next day (actually same day as it was after midnight), so it was probably a blessing in disguise at the time. That Mel Sykes though. What a lady.

And so the inevitable happened and the morning of the court case came and I was trying to prepare myself to take Oasis, my former good friends, to court. As I did this, I had the unnecessary negative vibes emanating from the Footballer who was pissed off with me for copping off with Miss Sykes. This guy was driving me to court and he had issues with me! He was there to give me moral support yet he was now doing the exact opposite.

He at least drove me there, and he walked with me into the court building. I was beginning to think that maybe he'd get past his issues and lend me some support after all; but all I can say is that he must have really liked Melanie Sykes, as after we got to reception, he turned around and walked away without another word. Walked out in the middle of my court case. That was the last I saw of him.

What a dick, I hear you say. Well, I can't comment on that.

So I found myself there, on my own, nervous as hell in the middle of London in the High Court.

'Mr. Ashbee to Room 1,' was announced from behind the huge and imposing reception desk. My stomach flipped, my mouth went dry. I swallowed with an audible click and then walked towards to the court room. This is it, I thought to myself. I was about to lock horns with Oasis. My old mates. My band. With a trembling hand, I pushed open the door marked 'Court Room 1'.

My visions of what things would look like that day were, I imagine, like most people's visions. A massive court room clad in dark wood; a judge in all his robes sat in a massive pulpit beneath a huge coat of arms on the wall. I'd proceed to stand in the dock, wringing my hands and saying my bit in front of various legal beagles, while artists drew pictures of me and an assembled crowd gasped at the tales of injustice that I was regaling them with. That's what any sane person would think, surely?

Instead, I walked in to six of Oasis's people sat with my one person, all gathered around a massive table. There was no sign of Noel, or of Liam, or any of the guys. There wasn't even a court room as such, but a room of suits with a judge sat at the end of it. I'd built it up in my head that it was going to be a grand affair, more official; but all it boiled down to was a few legal people round a table. It was the first of a few reality checks. Then the legal jargon started, and I couldn't make head nor tail of it.

'The aforementioned blah blah. The heretofore alias henceforth blah blah.' You know, that kind of thing. I'm pretty streetwise, and am clued in when it comes to most things; but that. It was all so complicated. They would use twenty long words where five simple ones would do.

The judge listened to it all intently, nodding knowingly and making occasional notes or glances over toward me. I couldn't really work out what he was thinking, and managed to suppress the overwhelming urge to jump over the table to read what he was writing down about me.

I hadn't checked the forecast that morning, but I'm quite sure that if I had, a storm with a high chance of bullshit would have been predicted to descend upon where I was sat. There was my guy going against their guys, and I was looking back and forth and trying to get a grip on how I was actually faring in it all. Then came a break. I like to think of it as half time. No oranges and pep talk from the captain. There was just Chris, my idiotic solicitor. Of course, at the time I hung on his every word.

He was smiling, laughing, ecstatic, buzzing, and said to me: 'You're going to win this, Paul.'

'You what?' I was stunned, as that wasn't what I'd got from the wave after wave of incomprehensible shite that had been washing over me in there.

'You're going to win it, you've got them. The judge is having it, he's on your side,' he proudly replied.

I was over the moon. I couldn't believe it was going in my favour, but if this Chris guy said it was, then what could go wrong? In an instant, I was on the phone to Mel Sykes telling her I was going to win. I was already planning to buy a house in London! I was even telling Mel I'd marry her, which would have been both awkward and news to my missus at the time. Still, in my mind I would probably invite Des O'Connor's son round for dinner with me and Mel, though, and everything. You know, I was on it. I was buzzing from Chris putting all my fears aside.

It. Was. Actually. Happening.

I was jumping round like a loon but still keeping it together as far as the legal lot were concerned. So next thing I knew, half time was over and we headed back into the room. Now, out of nowhere, there were two new geezers sat in there at the table with the rest of the Oasis legal team, and they were all murmuring among themselves. It would appear that Noel had had the nod that things weren't going his way and he'd made a phone call. Team A evidently weren't doing it properly, so he'd added Team B, who must have been on standby; so now he'd got a super team in place. These guys had apparently been legal people for Prince Charles, so they really were the dog's bollocks. That's how serious it got once they realised they couldn't do it on the cheap, when Noel got the call saying that I might actually get somewhere. Then, and only then, did he sit up and listen. And then he did what he was very well equipped to do: he threw money at it.

I found out afterwards that the whole thing would have cost Oasis about £150,000 to fight me in the court case. That's 150,000 pounds. Noel could have just thrown me £50k and we'd have all been done and dusted and he would have saved himself double that. But no, his pride wouldn't let that happen. And in the process, it was obviously all over the papers and their bad boy image was getting a lot of attention. It was in *The Sun*, it was in *The News Of The World*, *The Star*. The press were all over this and everyone was loving it – except me.

Well, Noel seemed to be getting his money's worth from where I was sat, because the two new additions pulled out the big guns. They went on the attack and hit the judge with a barrage of stuff that made him start questioning everything he'd been decided upon before the half time mark; everything that had seemed so positive.

After a while facing Noel's Legal SAS team and all the crap that they threw at him, the judge slammed his hammer down and said he wanted to talk to me in private. They all duly exited and the judge, who was a top bloke by the way, looked at me straight in the eye.

He said: 'Listen, lad. They've got you here. You deserve something out of this, and I don't like it. However, I can't award you anything. I want to, but I can't. All you needed was a signature.'

He knew. He was salt of the earth and he knew when an old skool gentlemen's agreement had been gone against, and in a court of law, that's pretty much what it came down to. We may as well have done a pinkie-swear as far as the system was concerned.

In all of the statements, no one denies anything in there, the things that I was attached to. They couldn't, as I'd been there and I'd done them. The thing is, they were saying I was a mate, and I was doing those things because I wanted to do them. Which of course I did. It was my dream first of all before anyone else's. But they'd twisted it into something else.

So there I sat, reeling. I had just gone from high as a kite, thinking I'd be getting the payout I deserved for everything that I had done, only to crash and burn, realising that I wasn't getting a thing. I was already on my arse with nothing to show for all my work and I realised I'd been kicked again while I was down. I'd only had the one chance of doing this with legal aid on my side, and the judge had essentially said that they had me by the balls. That was it. Or so I thought. There was to be a twist in the tale of Bigun versus Oasis.

Chapter Fifteen
When Love Breaks Down

In about 2002 Oasis were headlining at Lancashire Cricket Club, supported by Richard Ashcroft, who was playing solo after The Verve split three years earlier. It was a hell of a gig and I was going.

This all happened on a weekend when I was larging it up with the Man City football team (as you do), and I arrived in a massive stretch limo with them in the car park at the club. Me, Nicholas Anelka, Shaun Goater, Kevin Horlock and everyone was buzzing. We were a happy bunch of souls arriving for a happy time.

You see, since that kick in the teeth from the Oasis lads, I'd been getting on with things. I was grafting and making sure I was looking after my girls. I was building my empire and sorting my life out, getting back on track with the valeting with the help of Tony Mc.

So there we were, in party mode in a big fat stretch limo, big day out, and we rocked up ready to party and mad for it. I climbed out the limo and saw Liam clock me. My heart flipped as I didn't really know how this would go, as contact between us since the court case had been virtually non-existent. When we did talk, it was strained and changed, which was sad. But life goes on and went on.

I needn't have worried, not with Liam anyway, as he trotted up to me and took my hand and shook it. I could feel the electricity between us through that contact, like we'd always had in the old days. That bond. He asked where I was for the gig, and I told him we were on the balcony, basically hanging over the stage.

He kept it low key, obviously not wanting his brother to see what he was doing, and he seemed wary, checking out who was in the car with me. But he'd shaken my hand, and I appreciated that. You know, it was a gesture when he could have done nothing. He shook my hand, said nothing and buggered off again into the crowd.

I found out later that Liam went back in and said to Noel that I'd arrived there with all the Man City lot. Naturally, I'd recently cost him £150k plus and it wasn't sitting well with Noel that I was there at a gig that he was about to play. It didn't sit well at all. It would be strong for me to say he wanted his revenge, but I think it would be fair to say that he strongly didn't want me there.

We all filed up to our box, the box that I'd paid for, and we intended to get on it. Ironically, Noel wanted to get me off it. Now, this particular box and how the Lancashire Cricket Ground is set out means that we would be above them when they were on stage. More to the point, Noel always stands on the same side of the stage, the left side. That happened to be directly under the balcony where I was going to be stood, and naturally, after the outcome of the court case and with him knowing I'd have been simmering on things for a while, he was anxious to change that. We all knew what it meant. Oasis were within the range of a thrown bottle and Noel didn't like the idea very much.

So I assume that what Noel did was round up all of his security and send them my way. There I was, in the VIP box, and I'd just started on my first beer, a couple of mouthfuls in, and all hell broke loose. Brezhnev (my name for Noel) bowled in, sporting a full beard and glasses. He looked like an old bagger, not that he came close enough for me to inspect him.

He stood behind about ten of his henchmen, keeping his distance, which was the right thing to do with me after a few years of stewing over things. Before I realised what I was doing, I'd grabbed a chair ready to swing at him. I mean, there he was coming at me, but with an army to do his work for him. Well, needless to say that Noel's army didn't let me swing that chair. They just swamped me; I couldn't do anything about it or get near to our

Brezhnev. Six of them hauled me up into the air so that I was like a pinned insect, kicking and struggling. This was in front of all of my mates, in the box that I'd paid for. I was fuming.

'That'll fucking teach you, you bastard,' he said to me, or words to that effect.

'You fuck off,' was my succinct reply. Then I realised he was just laughing at me.

I lost it.

I was angry, I was embarrassed, and I was being held up by a ton of hired muscle. After all that had happened, I was being subjected to all of this!

I proceeded to explain to Noel for the purpose of clarity that it was advisable for him to desist with laughing and gloating, as he had reached the inevitable tipping point of my patience, whereby I was jolly angry and ready to bring down upon him an ire of biblical proportions.

It was something like that, anyway. There may have been a few more swear words, who knows.

Even the football players I was with were all up for bundling in. I'm glad they didn't now, as that would have been a very different outcome. But at the time, they were prepared to get stuck in, but Noel's hired muscle were like the SAS. They were in and out in seconds. It was so fast, all that was left of me was a spinning beer bottle with two sips taken out of it and a pair of sunglasses. That's what I like to think, anyway.

Of course, the press were there to see this unfolding drama and were to subsequently report on it. A sceptic could think he'd set it up for them to be there, to set the record straight and embarrass me. The press loved it. Oasis. Football stars. An ongoing feud. Bouncers. Violence. They were all over it.

In true Bigun style, I made it worse, of course. Because I'd seen red, and I mean I was bloody apoplectic with rage: when I was being held in the air, I was kicking, screaming and struggling. In the struggle I managed to clock one of them in the face with my elbow, and in the shock he let me go. That meant that where it had been an even balance of weight of this big man being held aloft, now the balance was no longer there.

So I fell. I fell when they'd just reached the stairs, so I fell on the stairs on my back. Man, that really hurt, but that was it, I'd broken the hold. Three of them let go and left me alone, but three still had me gripped.

I asked them to kindly relinquish their hold upon me. I also advised the London chap of the hired muscle who I knew from before that despite the venue, it really wasn't cricket that they were doing this.

This was Manchester. My town. You don't come into my town, and eject me from a VIP box that I'd paid for, and carry me out in front of my mates and everyone. Not without repercussions. I explained all of this to any of those musclebound bastards that cared to listen. Again, I may have said it differently at the time, but you get the gist of it.

The biggest thing of it all was how embarrassing it was for me. This was Oasis playing in Manchester and there were a lot of people there, and of course, they were watching me being manhandled out. The fans, the press, the security. If you've ever been at a gig and something's kicked off, then you know exactly what you do. You watch it like you would watch a football match or a fight in a ring. Only this time it was Paul Ashbee in the blue corner and a load of muscle in the pretty green corner.

So, having resigned myself to the fact that there wasn't much I could do right then, humiliated, and with tears in my eyes, I walked the longest walk of my life. All six of them stood in a line creating a corridor of muscle for me to skulk through, and cameras were clicking, people were watching. They all saw that I wasn't going to do anything as I wasn't able to do anything. I was like a caged tiger!

I like to think that the general feeling among those watching was echoed by the security guard as I reached the gate at the end of the corridor of hired muscle.

He looked at me right in the eye and said 'Fucking wankers, man.'

I told him that he probably didn't want to be around later, as I was going to bring a Mancunian hell down upon all those that had just publicly done me wrong. You see, earlier in my life, I'd been a football hooligan. You can lock that side of you away and hope that it never comes out, but believe you me, it's always there. And this day, I'd gone back twenty years to that time and I was in a rage of biblical proportions. I'd seen red. The red mist had descended and all I could think of was revenge.

This all happened so fast, but my mate Big Mark had seen it all unfold from the VIP box, and he had made his way down to me by now to see if I was OK. I assured him I was but told him what my intentions were and asked if he wanted in on the action. He did, and suggested we rally the troops and sort it later.

I'd like to think that I then managed to salvage some dignity from the whole surreal affair that had just unfolded. I whistled the limo, which hurtled over and screeched to a halt by me and in front of those still interested in what was going on. I cracked a bottle of champagne open and swigged from it as I proceeded to ring all of the troops to tell them what had happened, as we sped out of the grounds. I was ready to go to war, dear reader. I was out of control and in a rage.

So I met the lads in Denton. I was ready to do damage to save some face, to make myself feel better after another body blow from my old mates. What they did though was very different to what we would have done in the old days: they came up with something cunning. They talked me down. They talked sense to me.

They were right. They were telling me that this was who I had been, but I could no longer be. It wouldn't have achieved anything other than make things much worse for me and I would have probably ended up back inside - and for what? A bit of pride.

So what they did suggest was something that never would have crossed my mind before.

'Go to the police,' they said.

'YOU WHAT?' was my obvious reply. That hadn't even entered my head. Why would it?

'You've been assaulted. You were evicted from a private box that was yours for an allotted period of time. You paid for it, you did nothing wrong, and you got manhandled out of it. They can't do that.'

Well, they were right, of course. This wasn't what I wanted to do. I wanted to go down to The Lowry where they were all staying and smash stuff up like a Manc Hulk. I wanted to work my way through all of their security and do some serious damage with a gang of about 40 football hooligans. They were certainly up for it, and as far as I was concerned, it was over for Oasis.

Who knows what would have happened that night if I hadn't been talked down? And it was really down to one man and one man only. Boz.

He was the one that said, 'Don't. Think about it, Bigun. You'll end up getting nicked.'

'Yeah, you're right,' I said. If I could go back in time and tell the teenage football hooligan version of me that twenty odd years down the line he'd be going to the police to report the biggest rock and roll band in the world for assault, I'd never have believed it. Not for one minute. But that's what I did, and I'm so glad that I did it. Not for the financial gain, but more for the moral gain. My path would have taken a very different course if I'd gone on the rampage that my red mist was telling me to. I very much doubt I'd be where I am today if I'd succumbed to my primal urges.

So I went to the police. Willingly, which I think was a first for me. I went down to Old Trafford Police Station, and stepped up to the desk sergeant on the front desk.

'Hello, I'd like to report being assaulted by Noel Gallagher,' I told him, conspiratorially.

The guy just started laughing, and said, 'Excuse me, sir? The gentleman out of the band Oasis?'

I adamantly responded, 'Yeah, just over there,' and I started pointing to over the road.

The policeman looked at me thoughtfully, then assumed I'd been drinking and subsequently really didn't believe me. Then the banter started, and I explained I was The Bigun and I told him briefly what had happened earlier at the cricket ground. Then he finally started taking things seriously, and sat me down in one of the uncomfortable chairs in the waiting area, and before you know it a lady turned up ready to talk.

The policewoman took me in a room, and interviewed me meticulously, making sure she got all of the history of it and what it had ultimately escalated to. I'm pleased to say that they ended up taking it very seriously and they said, to my surprise, that they'd go and arrest him.

When it came to them actually arresting him though, he'd been clever. In my opinion, he'd been advised by his people and had got his brief on it already before they'd even turned up, so that meant that the story was watertight and prepared when the rozzers knocked on the door of wherever he was.

Of course, it turned out that they couldn't actually arrest Noel himself, as technically he hadn't laid a single one of those talented fingers on me. He'd ordered his muscle to, yes, but he was covered in Teflon as far as an assault charge was concerned against him personally. They interviewed him properly and everything, and he was a clever bastard.

The police told me that he'd said to them that he wasn't comfortable with me being there in close proximity to him, and that I'd made threats towards him and Bonehead. I explained that it was actually Bonehead that had threatened to get me shot, not the other way round. They said that they had it on record that Paul Arthurs had complained about me before, so that stuck another nail in the coffin! I hadn't even turned up at his house when he imagined that I had and that was when he threatened me AND went to the police saying that I was hassling him.

In addition, the police had been told by Noel that I was attention seeking and that I was doing it all for the press. I said they were the ones that started all that press nonsense back in 1994 when they went to the papers saying that I'd scratched Cantona's car; and we all know that ended up with me getting the sack. Liam brought my name to the table first and foremost, not me.

I explained how I'd then ended up on my arse, so that when the papers rang me and asked: 'Bigun, has Liam got a chocolate brown Rolls Royce?'

I said: 'Yeah.' Five hundred quid.

'Bigun, has Liam bought a giant seashell encrusted windmill that doubles as a matchbox holder?'

'Yes, Mr Sun Reporter, he has.' Another five hundred quid in my pocket.

I didn't work the press, they worked me. And there were times when they were the only source of income, when five hundred quid thrown at you for nothing would have been virtually impossible to turn down, over a period of about five years. But let it be said that I never chased it. Never. They had always approached me up until this point.

I'm sure at the time I must have seemed childish with the whole 'but it was them that started it, Miss!' business. But facts are facts. It was all a mess.

So now I realised how things were going, and I wasn't stupid. This was all working against me and I knew it. I also knew that if they'd dug further, there would be witnesses to his security pouncing on me and carrying me out forcefully, but not one person would have seen anything that could stitch Noel himself up. It would all be hearsay. I couldn't touch him. I was fucking furious, he'd sidestepped me again.

Of course, I got right on my high horse with my mates who'd talked up the right thing to do. 'I told you we should've gone and smashed them up! Now I'll never get at them.' I was gutted, but I hadn't given up. I walked out of that police station and I knew there had to be a way to get at them. You know, even if I could just piss them off a bit. So I decided that I'd fight fire with fire.

The Sun have always had their Bizarre feature pages, which have all the gossip of the time from the entertainment world. Back then there was always something about Oasis in it, and it had often been verified by me for the little injections of cash that were most welcome at a time of frugality. The writer for that feature was Dominic Mohan and I had his number.

So I rang him.

'Dom, I've just been assaulted by Oasis,' I said, and I could almost hear his ears prick up on the other end of the phone. 'Yeah, they threw me out of a VIP box at one of their gigs, I got all roughed up and I've just had them on the phone. They're settling for £25,000.'

Oh yes, I did.

And yes, they printed it. Did it piss them off? Oh very much so. Naturally Oasis got on the phone to them demanding that it be retracted and a full apology be printed otherwise they'd sue, which gave me a delicious little bit of satisfaction.

I'd played them at their game, using the press to big up their image, their bad boy side. At the time, off my head, I believed this was how they wanted me to play it, and play it I surely did.

In 2005 Oasis were on their *Don't Believe The Truth* tour and played the Etihad stadium. For those who don't know, the Etihad stadium is now the home of Manchester City Football Club and is a bit of a big deal. It seats 60,000 and is Mecca for all the Man City fans in and around Manchester. Oasis were setting another record with this gig, as at the time, it was the biggest stadium in the UK and th**ey** filled it. Of course they did!

Now, lots of water had passed under the bridge by the time this came about, and I was getting back on my feet since losing the court case but winning the assault case. So I was in a box with Michael Bray and Johnno Scott, who back in the day had got me into New Order.

We had a good drink, bit of the other. As the gig was going on, I realised that if I could get to them we'd have another fight and I'd be in the papers again. All the boxes were on the same corridor, so I could surreptitiously work my way through all the minimal security. So, despite being in a pretty good place, or possibly because of it, I found myself working my way round to get them.

So, I went through these people and I went through those people, and I eventually found myself literally in their hospitality suite. I noticed that people were clocking me and were thinking, 'Oh my God. It's Paul Ashbee', and obviously getting a bit nervous! Of course, they had no idea what mind frame I was in, whether I was angry or building bridges or what.

They were all looking at me, and I was looking at them. They were all looking at each other and probably wondering when all the security were going to arrive and when the titans were going to come off stage.

Obviously, I was loving all of this. Then I noticed there was a glass door and on the other side I could see Joey Barton. I asked to get my arm stamped so I could get back in easily. I got let through the door, so I didn't have to go all the way round. Now,

I'd known Joey for ages, and we started having a right old laugh, and he was introducing me to the people who didn't know me as the geezer that put Oasis together.

There was a boxer there that night, and all of a sudden he sidled up to me and said, 'Alright mate, have you got a minute?' He accompanied the question with the international sign language for 'step over here where people can't hear what I'm saying to you'. By this time, Johnno had joined me, as your mates do when they see something might be about to turn awkward.

I was like, 'You mean me?' wondering who the hell this was and what was going to happen here.

'The lads want to see you,' he replied mysteriously.

Obviously I enquired as to what lads this guy was representing, wondering if he meant the band, of course.

'Paul.'

'Paul who?'

'Paul Gallagher.'

I told him where to go, but he reassured and persuaded me to follow him, which I did. And what they did was as soon as I was through that glass door, they shut it and trapped Johnno the other side so that I was basically there on my own. I was set up like an idiot!

So I was facing the boxer, Bod and two Cockney Liam wannabees with ridiculous copycat haircuts. There were others, and they were all the people that I no longer knew, all the hangers on, the pretenders. There was a wall of anger in my face from the entourage that used to be me!

'You're not wanted 'ere. Get out,' they advised me.

'You get me out,' was my succinct and mature reply, challenging them.

Now, I'm not a small man. I'm 6'5' of prime Manchester meat, but I have a big mate. So big in fact, that even I call him 'Big Mark'. He's touching 7 foot tall and a proper Viking. And he showed up at this point out of nowhere, and was very welcome, I can tell you. Don't get me wrong, I can have a go in any situation, and it's what's got me in problems before; but there were six or seven of this lot fronting up to me and Big Mark was back up I could well do with, if it all turned nasty.

And it could. I was all psyched up now and ready to go. I challenged them to get me out, bolstered by the humungous Viking at my side, who I knew would have my back. He's always been like a guardian angel to me, Big Mark has; and him turning up there out of the blue is no exception to the rule. He always seems to pop up when I need him most, when the shit hits the fan. And right now it looked like someone had lined up a massive silver fan and somewhere a big pile of shit was about be thrown at it.

Well, Big Mark was getting up into people's faces, and I was too. There was lots of 'come on, then' and 'you come on.'

With it being a hospitality area at a gig, you tended not to get to drink out of glass items. This is for obvious reasons, such as if a fight were to occur between two rival parties. As if! Meanwhile, this safety measure was proving fortuitous for Bobby Langley, as somehow, in my fury, my aim was spot on and I managed to launch a plastic pint glass perfectly into his face. God knows what would have happened if it was a proper glass, as I certainly didn't pause to think!

Yeah, I'd lost it. I'd seen red. What got me most was that all these hangers on were all wannabees and I was an original. They all wanted to lick the arses of Oasis and take me on, yet I could guarantee that none of them would be there in a year's time. So what do you do in these situations? You paraphrase Oasis songs at them. Oh yeah.

I was pointing and shouting 'Who are you? Who ARE you? Where were you while these lot were getting high? Where were you while I was getting high with them?'

I was offering them all up. I would have if Big Mark hadn't been there, but with him there as well I was invincible. I was pointing. I was beckoning. 'Come on then. Come on!'

I was raging, dear reader. Raging. And I can honestly say that they were shitting it. Bricking it. Scared.

It infuriated me beyond words. I couldn't believe that in front of me was this bunch of hangers on, with their copycat hair, copying the guy that I'd introduced to the whole music scene. The guy that I'd coerced and cajoled into trying out for the band. I was ready to do some damage and they knew it. They were outnumbering us two to one by this stage, but still none of them approached; because they knew.

Big Mark may be big, but he isn't stupid. He could see where this was all going and it wasn't going to end up well whichever way you sliced it. Either I would have done some damage and we would have both been nicked and there'd be injuries and lawsuits and who knows what. I'd been grafting too hard to get my life back on track and he didn't want to see me put all of that to waste. Obviously, the other way it could've gone was with them battering the hell out of us - after all there was a boxer there as well - but it didn't reach that stage.

'Come on, mate. I'm getting you out of here,' Big Mark said to me, and with me still pointing, shouting and misquoting Oasis lyrics at my would-be assailants with their copycat hair, he put his arm around me and led me out of the hospitality suite and away from trouble. He was probably the only man that could do that when I was in the middle of the red mist that I was seeing, but I thank him for that.

Anyway, he manhandled me down the stairs, out the back of the stadium and into the back of a Range Rover, and we sped off.

This is how it became, and it was beginning to get boring. I knew I couldn't go through life constantly chasing them: they'd always have people around them or security protecting them. It was like they were in control, and that made me feel out of control. I didn't like that one bit. But as the years had passed, it had become like a game of cat and mouse; and I was never going to get to the end of that game.

It was sad, but it was a turning point for me. I could have just faded away then. Slide away, even. But if I had, I wouldn't have gone on all the other adventures that were to come.

Thinking back now, now that so much water has gone under the bridge, I wonder what I would have done if I'd got near to them. I was clinging on to a rage that didn't need to be there any more, when maybe I just wanted to see my old mate. Not to have a go, or throw a punch. I just wanted have a bear hug and to have a laugh talking shit with him again. Fortunately, many years later, it got back to that.

Chapter Sixteen
Super Mario

I had been getting messages from Liam about meeting up and burying our differences. I was all for it but felt that once a relationship had been spoilt then it was nigh on impossible to fix.

I wasn't working but Liam's contact had revived old enthusiasm. That coupled with the Sky Sports news banner excitedly announcing 'Breaking News' as it scrolled along the bottom of my TV screen. I was sat at home feeling a little bit under the weather. I sniffled and waited in anticipation as it revealed over and over again that Mark Hughes had been appointed the manager of Manchester City Football Club. I suddenly felt a little bit better.

I had always got on well with Mark Hughes, who is a proper 'man's man'. For all the seriousness and steely eyed determination in his role as a football manager he genuinely liked nothing more than a good giggle, and I gave him plenty. I decided to give him a day to settle in and then make a phone call.

The following morning I was on the blower nice and early.

'Morning Sparky and welcome back to Manchester my mate,' I said in my most positive tones.

'Who the fuck is this?' came back his rather suspicious Welsh ones. Not at all what I expected. So, in mock indignant outrage I continued.

'Unbelievable Sparky, I can't even begin to tell you how insulted I am. It's only Bigun, the man who put the 'Man' in Manchester.'

Hughesy paused and then laughed as he recognised who I was and soon we were talking like it was The Cliff in 1992. I explained my situation and asked if there was any chance of being re-employed at City. Hughesy asked me to give him a few days to look over the operation and then told me he would get back to me. That was good enough for me, and a couple of days later, true to his word, he was back on.

'Right Bigun, you're to be at the Carrington training ground, first thing in the morning.'

'No problem Boss!'

Yes. Get fuckin in there my son. I'm back with the Blues.

The following morning I was at the Carrington Training Complex with two of the cleanest and most professional looking vans in the northern hemisphere. First impressions count, and City had a new owner, namely Thaksin Shinawatra, the former Prime Minister of Thailand, and I was out to impress.

I had erected my marquee and I laughed as one by one the players arrived. It was all back slaps from the players I already knew, and I gave the players I didn't a warm and hearty Mancunian welcome.

'Welcome to the wonderful world of The Bigun.' Most laughed, a few didn't, and one or two looked downright petrified, but at least some sort of impression was left.

There was a good feeling around this City team. They were a talented bunch and full of personality, which always leads to a good team spirit. I think you can underestimate just how important morale is to the success of a football team.

There was also a good feeling around the company. We provided a class one service that involved not only ensuring the players could see themselves in the reflection of their vehicle's paintwork but also sorting any other 'issues' that might arise. Life was on the up and I needed to make sure it stayed that way.

Now I wouldn't consider myself pessimistic, but I must say that as soon as I seem to take stock of my life and find myself nearing contentment it doesn't seem to last for long. And lo and behold one cold and wet Saturday evening in December, City decided it was time to spin the merry go round once more and sack Mark Hughes.

Personally, I didn't think this was justified. Hughesy had built a good team at City and in my opinion his signing of Carlos Teves and Vincent Kompany provided the pivotal moment in the transformation of City's fortunes.

I called at Hughesy's house a couple of days later with a little gift for him. Just a way to say thank you for helping me out.

And so as soon as they'd cleared the stained mug and mouse mat from Mark Hughes's desk there was a new man rolled in. And that man turned out to be the former Italian international, Roberto Mancini. I knew he'd played with Savage at Leicester so was straight on to Sav for the heads up.

'He's a great bloke Bigun, you two will get on like a house on fire.'

'More a cottage on fire in your case Sav, you Welsh melt.'

'Right, I'm gonna tell him a few stories about you to make sure he knows what you're about.'

'Don't be doing that Sav.'

That's how it is with Robbie, he's a good character.

So, there was a new manager, and with him a new set of backroom staff. I laughed and remembered that things could be a lot worse. Unfortunately, what I believed to be a positive aspiration turned instead into a prediction. Mario Balotelli arrived.

Mario Balotelli flew into Manchester in 2010 shortly after appearing on Italian television sporting an AC Milan shirt. Not surprisingly, it didn't go down too well with the fans of Inter Milan, the team that Mario actually played for and which paid his wage. Jesus, could you imagine Aguero appearing in Red or Rooney in Blue? There'd be riots.

My first encounter with the fully-fledged lunatic came on an otherwise dull Friday. Mario had managed to write off the first car that City had provided and had been given a replacement Audi Q7 so he could bob around Manchester. It had taken him less than two days to start his now legendary ballooning about and I reckon the alarm bells started to ring around the club as soon as he arrived; and to be honest, they never really stopped.

I was stood in the Carrington car park when I heard the full throttle of an engine followed by a scream of tyres. I stood frozen to the spot as a vehicle hurtled through the car park gates and towards me. It shuddered to a halt, spewing a cloud of Mancunian dust and grit into the air. I spat, and as my sphincter settled the window of the vehicle lowered to reveal a quite placid Mario Balotelli, chewing a toothpick and smiling.

'Where you want me?'

Still a little bit shell shocked I simply pointed to the allocated spot.

With a wink over his sunglasses he threw the huge vehicle into reverse and wildly swung towards the space. Unfortunately for James Milner, his BMW X5 had been the previous job and sat next to where Mario intended parking.

As he pulled into the spot, I could hear the scrape and buckle of metal as he caught James Milner's Beemer. I grimaced as Mario simply hopped out and gave me another huge smile. I waited for an apologetic reaction from him for the damage caused, but instead he simply sauntered past me. His quiet chuckle turned into a roar as he reached the clubhouse. In absolute wonderment I laughed, which in turn made Mario laugh even louder.

Now normally it would be my responsibility to explain to Mr Milner just how his car had been trashed, but fortunately for me Shawn Wright-Phillips had also witnessed the coming together and it wasn't long before a rather angry Mr Milner appeared in the car park. As he came towards me, he saw his wounded BMW sat with the bumper hanging off.

'What the fuck happened?' he asked angrily. I played it like Switzerland and stayed neutral, as I considered this probably the safest option.

'I'm not the man to answer that.'

Jimmy simply glowered at me.

This was my first ever encounter with Mario, and after it I sat shaking my head. There haven't been many people in my life that have thrown me, but this guy was another league. I guess I admired his carefree attitude and his rebellious spirit. I'd seen it before in a young friend from Burnage. Mario really did not give a flying and was only interested in having a bit of fun.

We would meet most days and enjoyed each other's company. I offered to cage fight him, which he agreed to. There was not a chance I would go through with it, but I enjoyed winding him up.

Early one afternoon I was taking a bit of time out when I received a phone call.

'Hey, big guy, it's Mario.'

'Hey, crazy guy, it's Bigun not big guy. Just you remember who I am round here.'

Always best to give back to Mario to let him know he's not always in charge.

'You clean my car for me. I'm at a hotel, you need to come now.'

Guess he wasn't getting the 'you're not in charge' bit.

So I headed off towards The Hilton in Manchester City Centre. Certain jobs I like to attend personally rather than send a crew, and with Mario you were always likely to encounter an adventure. As was becoming the norm, he did not disappoint.

It was blustery and cold, and Mario was on his day off. I entered through the side reception of the hotel and made a beeline for the concierge's desk.

'Hiya pal, I'm here for Mr Balotelli's car keys.'

The elderly and red eyed concierge stood in a day-old shirt and decade-old waistcoat, grimacing at the sound of Mario's name. He closed his eyes and in an almost defeated manner croaked out, 'I have not got Mr Balotelli's car keys, nor have I been able to contact Mr Balotelli's room...' - he glanced at his watch - '...for the last seven hours.'

He pointed towards the front of the hotel, where I spotted Mario's car parked erratically across the entrance. Taxi and delivery drivers were all sitting looking rather unhappy as only one vehicle at a time could manage to squeeze past Mario's motor.

I asked if he'd tried ringing him on his mobile, and his eyes widened as if to say, 'what do you fucking think?' I was thinking he might be tired but there was seriously no need to be so fuckin sarky, as I tried Mario's mobile myself. I rang him a couple of times and then texted. No answer; he was off the radar.

I decided to take a look at his car to see if there were any clues to where he might be.

I marched out towards the vehicle, which warranted warrior-like looks from the impatiently waiting drivers. I ignored them and cupped my hands as I peered through the tinted windows. As I slowly focused the most immediate thing that came to sight was a set of car keys conveniently sat in the car's ignition. The vehicle must have been worth a hundred grand but hey, in Mario's world, people don't steal. I was thinking that maybe he was right after I opened the car door. Sticking out the arm rest, resting on the front seat, and filling up the passenger foot space were hundreds of notes. The ten, twenty and fifty kind.

I shook my head and laughed as I removed the keys, locked the motor and to a barrage of questions and abuse from the waiting vehicles I headed back inside. I collared the concierge and together we returned.

The concierge first took the time to placate the waiting traffic and then stood and shook his head as I showed him the cash. We quickly bundled it together and neatly sorted it into different envelopes the concierge had brought along. In total it was just short of twenty grand. The concierge had me sign a declaration confirming such and left.

Now maybe I should have moved the car, but a job is a job so before I did I headed for the van. When I returned to Mario's vehicle, I had to explain to the waiting angry line of traffic, 'It's a crime scene, I'm with CSI.'

I then fetched my hand held car cleaning kit and with my surgical mask strapped on I set about an interior car clean.

When I returned with my hand held vacuum the mood got even darker, so I lifted the vacuum for the impatient drivers to see and told them, 'Collecting fibres.'

I was nearing the end of the valet and thinking I'd done a good deed for Mario. Just as such pleasant thoughts were running through my mind there was a strange sensation in my left buttock which, with my right buttock, was poking out the back of the motor as I cleaned.

The strangely cold sensation suddenly became fiery hot and I screamed in pain. I then compounded my pain by smashing my skull against the door frame of the car as I pulled myself out in a panicked hurry. I spun round, one hand pawing at my arse, the other on my head. The pain was excruciating, and I howled.

Then I realised that standing in front of me was Mario. With a pin and an insane grin. I raised my left hand away from my arse and there was blood.

'What the fuck? You've stabbed me!' I spluttered.

I was struggling to comprehend what was going on and it became too much for me; I boiled over.

'Put the pin down dickhead and we'll sort this out toe to toe.'

The anger had taken over. You can't just poke a pin in me and not expect repercussions. I was game for kicking right off. Mario realised such and actually looked shocked and hurt by my reaction! He was too fuckin much.

'I'm sorry Bigun. Are you hurt?'

The anger was knocked off the boil. I felt the wound and it was only small.

'You're a fuckin mental job aren't you Mario? Lucky for you it's not deep.'

Mario sighed and the tension was removed from the air in a breath. I calmed down and then started to giggle. Mario joined in and before long we were both roaring together. The waiting traffic looked on in disbelief.

'Listen, you can't walk round the streets of Manchester sticking people Mario. You gonna end up in the fucking clink.'

'I only stab people I like,' he replied.

And I actually felt proud. I'd been stabbed by Mario because he liked me! That's the type of effect Mario has on people. I suddenly remembered the money.

'Why have you left your car open and full of money? Can you do that in Milan? Because you sure as fuck can't in Manchester.'

'What money?' he responded, genuinely confused, until he realised and then smiled. 'Oh, I forget.'

I guess when you earn hundreds of thousands each week, twenty thousand pounds turns into loose change. Mario didn't even ask how much there was, which gives you an idea of what that huge amount of money meant to him. But he knew he was in safe hands with me. I had displayed my code of conduct, my duty of care. The Bigun looks after you full time not part time.

And so, after returning his money and getting stabbed in the arse I became the liaison between Mario and Mancunia.

I picked up Mario's car one Friday. I gathered up the twenty to thirty parking tickets that were strewn like confetti inside, and handed them over to Marco, his bodyguard, to pay. Marco shook his head and muttered in Italian, then rolled his eyes towards heaven dramatically. I was thinking that Manchester City Council should give Mario the key to the city for the amount of revenue he generated when the man himself appeared on the car park, fresh from training.

He smiled when he spotted us and immediately went to his boot, from which he retrieved five or six large boxes and plonked them at my feet.

Then, without any explanation or even a 'ciao' he simply gave Marco a nod to jump in and they both roared out of the car park leaving me and the boxes.

I stood and inspected the boxes. Anyone else, I would have been tearing them open like a child on Christmas morning, but this was Mario. Like a member of the bomb squad I gently prodded the box with my foot. Actually, this is probably a technique not used by the bomb squad. When I felt confident that there wasn't a surprise in store I opened a box.

It was filled with top notch Nike training clobber. I was impressed. I opened the rest of the packages to find the same and was as happy as Larry. It wasn't hooky, so I had a load of new clobber, all above board. I texted Mario to thank him and headed home.

Later that evening there was a knock on my front door. I peeped through the spy hole to see the weirdly enlarged and bulbous head of a City official. For some strange reason I started to wonder what Vincent Kompany would look like through a spy hole, but the thought was overcome by a feeling of dread. No phone call from the Club yet one of their officials was stood on my doorstep? I was thinking it was not good news.

I swung the door open and beamed, 'Hello, can I help you?'

The suit-wearing City representative shifted nervously from foot to foot.

'Can I have a word, Paul?'

'Yeah, man. What is it?' I replied, as that feeling of impending doom sank further.

'You're not allowed to accept any gratuities or gifts from the players as this contravenes Club regulations.' I reckon no matter what the Suit said it would be said in this smug manner.

'Do you mean the training gear from Mario?'

'Yes.'

'Well, you need to take that up with Mario, don't you?' was my kneejerk reply, and immediately I regretted it.

'Fair enough,' came the equally curt answer from the Suit, who then turned on his heels and purposefully strode off. I guess he had what he came for.

There I go again. Rather than simply placating the man, as I should have done, I had created an issue. But I also understood what the real problem was.

The official Club Liaison Officers did not like the fact that the players and their families relied on me to help them out. I guess they felt threatened, although on most occasions what I was doing for the players didn't even fall under the Club's remit anyway. The liaisons didn't want me there and they were waiting for an opportunity. I had a sneaky feeling I might have just provided one.

Early the next morning there was a call from Mario that proved my fears were well justified.

'You been a bad boy Bigun.' He laughed.

'What now?'

'I can't give you any more presents. They have told me. So, I have decided that I'm going to give you a present every day!'

'Thank you but no thank you, Mario. Just leave it, please. I'm sure somebody will want to speak to me, and I'll sort it then.'

Jesus, I didn't want to get involved in one of Mario's fights. Mario didn't know that he was doing wrong, and he certainly wouldn't stitch you up like that. He was just being his natural and generous self, so I was a bit put out by how these events had unfolded, and the fact my card had been marked by something that was just a throwaway gesture. I always acted with the Club's best interest at heart and more often than not fixed the issues that might have caused them a problem or two. But hey, such is life.

That morning the Club Liaisons informed the players that when it came to getting their cars cleaned, they would now have to drive their vehicles to the furthest part of the training complex and then walk back. It seemed that they had relocated my valeting pitch and informed everyone else but myself. I thought there was no way it'd work; these guys were used to people pandering to them. But this was the least of my problems.

I turned up at Carrington, to be told of my immediate move.

'No problem,' I lied, and headed over to the far side of the complex.

I then watched as the players pulled into the distant car park. Mario hammered into the car park as if he was being pursued and then slammed to a halt in my old valeting spot. Even from this distance I could hear the continuous blare of his car horn as he sat there in a one-man protest.

Soon the car was surrounded by confused Club Liaison officers and I watched as Mario exited the vehicle and remonstrated before abandoning his motor and storming off to the changing rooms.

Mario, being the guy he was, had got wound up by some actual rules being enforced in his charmed life, and had taken it upon himself to dig his heels in. I couldn't stop him even though I very much wanted to.

Shortly after this scene I was handed eight sets of car keys by Jerome Boateng. So now I could simply drive the cars over and then return. It was a small victory in a battle I didn't even want to be involved in but a nice touch by the players.

Mario approached me after the training session.

'Bigun, I have something for you,' he smiled as he handed me his car keys.

'Standard clean?'

'That is up to you. I am giving you the car. It is now yours, but you'll have to take me to a garage to get a new one.'

Unfuckinbelievable. He was now offering me a Maserati that must have been worth a cool quarter million. I laughed as I considered the reaction of the Club Liaison officers if I did accept this offer; but it was against my rules, so I couldn't.

'You are truly fuckin loco aren't you Mario? As much as I appreciate the gesture you know that I can't.'

For the next three days I was hounded by the man. He booked me flights to Mexico which he had to cancel at a cost, he left a Rolex that was worth lord knows how much in my van's glove compartment, which I returned, and he even offered to pay off my mortgage.

Day in, day out, he made a point of trying to give me stuff and all his efforts were relayed humorously around the Club. Mario wanted to piss off those who had tried to control him, those who worried about me getting too close, and piss them off he did. It was the beginning of the end.

Mario hadn't done it for any reason other than to stick up for me. He'd seen an injustice occurring, and he'd done what he thought was right. It backfired. The guy is crazy and passionate and a superb human being. He's still playing great football and I'm sure he'll continue to remain in the headlines for both good and bad reasons.

Afterword

This book has been a long time in the making, and it's been difficult to decide what to put in and what to leave out - I don't want to be negative about anything that happened and I don't want to upset anyone. I had some great times, the best. I'm older and wiser and I've put all the anger behind me.

I'm still Oasis' biggest fan; for me, it's all about the music. I've seen Liam a couple of times over the years and we've sorted out our differences. I genuinely have no hard feelings about all that happened. What I can say is that I'm proud of my input back then and wish all of them all the love in the world.

I've picked myself up and got on with life - and life is going well. My newest venture is opening a wine bar on King St in Manchester, backed by my old mate Georgi Kinkladze. Georgian wine is amazing, the oldest in the world, and we're starting a new Georgian Revolution right here in Manchester.

There are loads of people I want to thank - I just hope I've remembered them all, and I apologise to anyone I've left out - here goes...

My family of course, my daughters Lois, Lauren, Emily and Lilly, my mother and father Jean and Barry, Suzanne and Gaynor my sisters, Sav and Ged my grandchildren Sienna, Jayden and Hallie, my nephew and nieces Laura, Stephen and Beth, Jack and Josh, my cousins, Matt, Kay, Amie, uncle Harry and Andrea, Hilary and Keith, Haley and Phil, my Uncle Stuart RIP, my lifelong friends Mike Lester, John Scott, John Morrin, Jimmy Regan, Dave Rayson, Phil Mclean, Griff, the Cookson family, John Reagan, Mark Sherwod, the Morrin family, Dave Ellis, Slick Rick, Antony Dolan, Heath and Jason Watson, the Hegartys, Karina Aslund, Mike Tate, Sandy and Jackie, Dave Bosam, Mandy Rowan, Joel and Arron, the Rowan family, Big Kev and Michelle Doyley, Paul Hewitt, the Dolan Family, and of course Ricy fantastic, Tony Mac, Janine Martin, Kurt, Mizan, Bobby Bates, Cerice, Shelia, Louise Seal, Vicky Robson and Paige, Darren

Robson, Karen Little, Craig W, Warren, Simon Heaton, Ricky Hatton, Marcus the Main cat, Lisa and the kids, Big Kev, everyone at Taurus, John Macken, Browny, Jeff and Jim Whitley, Kevin Horlock, Robbie Savage, Lee Crookes, Micky Gray, Nicky Summerbee and Mike Summerbee, Chapey, Terry John, Fitzroy Simpson, Anton Forrester, Elliot Rocco James Hooper, Darrel, Chris Johnston, Chris and Tony Griffiths, Coatsey, Wayne Hewlet, Mark Chaisty, Warren Fisher, Eric Fisher and family, big Ray, Stephen Gareth Carol and Gwilym Davis, Kev Kavanna, Rose Morgan, Degsey and family, Micky Mellons, Keith Hill, Keith Curle, Mark Robbins, Paul the chairman and family and all at Radcliffe Borough, Dave and Gary Flitcroft, Peter Frith and family, Granty, Chris Samba, George, Scotty, Eric Scrag, Tash Toland, John Barrett, Lee Mall, Peter Barnes, Jeff Millward, Big Heath, Terry Corless, Lesley Gray, Terry Harkin, Colin Woodhead, Andrew Wallen, Hutchy, Yardy, Andrea McArthur, Georgina M, Degsey Williamson, Paul Buller, Joanne White, Jimmy Oakes, and to friends that are no longer with us, RIP Dave Tian, Brian Griffin, Terry Devlin, John Noble, Vinny Colins, Kevin Woodhead and Joanne Copeland.

Live Forever,

The Bigun.